D0390438

HIROSHIMA TWINS

THE TRUE STORY OF A GROUND ZERO FAMILY

FUMIKO TAKAHASHI

© 2022 Takahashi Planning Co. / Fumiko Takahashi / Tenbosha Publishing

All rights reserved. No part of this book may be reproduced or used in any manner without the prior written permission of the copyright owner, except for the use of brief quotations in a book review.

v10.31

Table of Contents

Remember this:

Even the most impossible parts of this story… really happened.

PART ONE

DETONATION

The action of causing an explosive device to discharge.

1
SECONDS

On May 9th, 1945, one of the first of fifteen B-29s built to function as a nuclear weapon delivery aircraft was on the assembly line at the Nebraska, USA factory. While still being outfitted, Colonel Paul W. Tibbets Jr., commander of the 509th *Composite Group*, chose it for the mission assigned to him. When finished, the Superfortress Bomber was flown to the Wendover Army Airfield, Utah, on June 14th. On June 27th, the yet-to-be-named plane was flown to Guam where it received bomb-bay modifications. On July 5th, it was flown to Tinian, one of the three islands in the Northwest Pacific Ocean, six-hours flying time from Japan.

During preparations for the first atomic mission in history, Colonel Tibbets took command of the aircraft and named it after his mother, Enola Gay Tibbets. Private Nelson Miller painted the name *Enola Gay* just under the pilot's window. Tibbets later recalled:

"At the time of deciding what to name the aircraft, my thoughts turned to my courageous red-haired mother, whose quiet confidence had been a source of strength to me since boyhood, especially during the soul-searching time when I decided to give up a medical career to become a military pilot.

At a time when Dad had thought I had lost my marbles, my mother had taken my side and said, 'I know you will be all right, son.'"

The 4,500 kg atomic bomb named *Little Boy* was loaded into the Enola Gay unarmed in case the plane crashed on take-off. On August 6th, at 2:40am, Colonel Tibbets and the crew of eleven prepared to taxi the plane. So photos could be taken, the runway was illuminated by floodlights. Tibbets leaned out the window to direct bystanders out of the way. On request, he gave a friendly wave to cameras.

The plane took off at 2:45am, August 6, 1945, heading for Iwo Jima. From there, they planned to set a course to Japan. Once they arrived over Hiroshima, they would arm Little Boy, drop it from an altitude of 9,470 meters at 8:15am Japan time.

It was estimated that it would take 43 seconds to fall nearly six miles to 600 meters: it's detonation height.

2
MIDORI

Midori Naka was a well-known stage actress in Japan. She became popular in 1935. On June 7, 1945, she and her nine-member acting troupe had moved to Hiroshima to perform during the summer season. They were there to boost morale by performing plays for workers in munitions factories.

They rented a house that was located 650 meters from the Enola Gay's target: *Ground Zero*. She was 36 years old.

3
NEEDLES

"People of Hiroshima, attention," came the voice of a radio announcer. It was midnight, eight hours before detonation. "Two-hundred American B-29s are approaching Southern Honshu. It is advised that the people of Hiroshima evacuate the city and head toward their designated *safe areas*."

The 45-year-old Yaichi Nakamura, kept the radio low so as not to disturb his wife and eight childrens' sleep. The ten members of the Nakamura family were:

Father Yaichi (45)

Wife Taeko (41)

Daughter Hisako (19)

Son Tamotsu (17)

Daughter Shizue (14)

Daughter Tsuneko (12)

Son Yutaka (9)

Daughter Fumiko (4)

Daughter Hiroko (4 mo.)

Daughter Aiko (4 mo.)

The decision to stay or leave the city was a constant worry for him these days. The Japanese cities that remained unharmed by American's wrath were diminishing, making the odds of Hiroshima being bombarded increase with each sunrise.

Yaichi, as well as most Japanese, knew that the likelihood of defeat in the fourth year of the war was strong. Indeed, large, and small cities in Hiroshima's Chugoku region had been hit by enemy bombs. Okayama, Kure, Otake, Tokuyama, Ube, cities that surrounded Hiroshima, had all suffered under the wings of B-29s, leaving only Hiroshima, the largest city in the area, unharmed. Why had its 350,000 residents been spared that horror? No one could say.

In the last year, the city's inhabitants had been actively evacuating buildings. Government pamphlets distributed to residents told of how to prepare for air raids, make bomb shelters, and much more.

The city's medical personnel were forbidden to leave. Teams of doctors, dentists, nurses, and pharmacists were on hand to help after an air raid. There were neighborhood civil defense teams that would assist with firefighting. Yaichi was on one of those teams.

Many families had been preparing for attacks by digging their own air-raid shelters. Yaichi and his family had also dug out shelter in their garden, praying to never need it.

Their shelter was four-meters deep, shored up by wood beams, with a three-meter dirt-mound on top of it. A narrow door was put on the entrance. The four-by-five-meter space wasn't much room for Yaichi's nine family members, but it would protect them from bombs that didn't come too close to it. But for sure, Yaichi worried about *too close* as well as *direct hit*.

So far, the Nakamura's prayers for no attacks had been answered. For some reason, large formations of B-29s never appeared in the sky of Hiroshima. Sometimes, one or two aircraft appeared like lost children, and an air raid warning was issued. By the time the sirens went off around the city, the sound of the plane's engines would diminish, then cease.

When will it be Hiroshima's turn? Yaichi thought as he turned off the radio and walked through his small sewing needle factory, on the way to his futon. *When will the B-29s come in hordes, piloted by the awakened giants filled with a terrible resolve? Will they be saying 'Remember Pearl Harbor' as their hands pull levers that release the fire to descend on us?*

Yaichi's family-owned needle manufacturing shop was located in the Misasamachi area of Hiroshima, one of the leading commercial and industrial areas in Hiroshima City. The streets were lined with shops and warehouses for wood, indigo, iron castings, glass, and vinegar. The needle-making industry was especially active in this area. The needles manufactured here were called *Hiroshima Needles*, with Yaichi's neighborhood being the number one needle-making area in the Orient.

Yaichi's *Nitto Needle Shop* was also his family's residence. He mainly hired local mothers to work there and subcontracted the polishing of the needles to other shops.

Hiroshima sewing needles have a tradition of 300 years, beginning in the early *Edo Period.* The Chugoku Mountains, which overlooks Hiroshima, is a major iron-sand producing area. Much of the iron produced was stored in Hiroshima Castle as the whole area prospered with the demand for needles. By the 1930s there were more than 200 needle-producing companies, large and small.

Now as the war was nearing its end, it became difficult to obtain even the fabric, let alone the iron material needed for uniform making. Most needle-making mills were closed, except for some major factories. The beginning of the war made the needle business prosper, now the war's ending made them languish.

Yaichi's *Nitto Needle Mill* was now also almost non-operational. For that reason, Yaichi joined the labor service corps in the town and was devoting himself to road maintenance and building evacuations. He pondered the fate of his once prosperous factory as he laid down on the futon next to his wife, Taeko.

They were married 19 years ago, when she was 22. Yaichi was four years older. Closing his eyes, he wondered if they would be blessed with more years. And if so, what would those years be once the war was over? Once the enemy set foot on Japanese soil.

The emperor had warned of the devastation that would come if the American barbarians ever came to their shores. Indeed, women had been trained to fight to the death with *naginata* spears, should that happen. What would he and his family be asked to do once the savages landed?

Taeko, now 41 years old, was born into the long-established Wada family at the western end of Hiroshima City. They lived in a soy sauce brewing shop owned by her father Tamajiro on prestigious land that was handed down for generations. Taeko's grandfather, Kichizaemon Wada, was a known celebrity of sorts. He was praised for donating his private fortune to help many local people in the turbulent times of the 1870s. A stone monument was erected to honor Kichizaemon's humanitarianism. Taeko always spoke with great pride about her grandfather.

A year after Yaichi and Taeko were married, their eldest daughter Hisako, now 18 years old, was born. Two years later, their son Tamotsu, now 19, then their daughter Shizue, now 14, and then their third daughter Tsuneko, now 12.

Soon after, came another son Yutaka, now 9. Their fourth, Fumiko, was born in 1941 when the war with America began. She was now four years old.

Four years later, in the spring of 1945, the couple unexpectedly had identical twin sisters. They were born at midnight on March 30th. Due to an air-raid warning, the lights in the house were turned off, so the world greeted the twins in candlelight.

The twins were in a breech position, but Taeko's aunt delivered them safely. Yet, they were small and weak. The remaining hot water needed was from the family bathtub. In the words of the famous movie-character Tora-San, in the movie *Otoko wa Tsuraiyo,* "Using the hot water from the Teishakuten Temple for new-born babies is lucky."

Later Taeko said, "I didn't want any babies until the war was over. In that time of extreme poverty, our family of eight didn't need two more milk drinkers, but we celebrated their birth anyway."

The aunt said, "When I saw the two cute babies with crisp eyes shining brightly, I told Taeko, 'Twins are *children of good fortune,* so raise them carefully.'"

After some thought, the couple gave these two precious lives the names Hiroko and Aiko. Hiroko meaning *Large.* Aiko meaning *Love.* Together, they were a wish for peace for all humankind. The twin babies were indeed raised as *children of good fortune*, the idols of a large family.

4
DETONATION

At 7am, on August 6, 1945, the Nakamura family stopped only momentarily preparing for their day as they heard the city siren sound off with a series of intermittent blasts. It was a warning of a possible air attack. This happened often enough that, though disconcerting, the family continued their morning activities.

An hour later, the *all-clear* sounded as a single Japanese weather plane made its daily flight over Hiroshima. The signal that there was no immediate danger for his family did little to alleviate Yaichi's fears as he left his home to join the city's maintenance group. *If an attack is not coming now,* he thought. *When will it?* Hopefully the war would end soon enough to keep his city the calm peaceful place it used to be.

Yaichi's eldest daughter, 19-year-old Hisako, was about to go to work at the Hiroshima Shinkin Bank. She had just started working there that spring.

Years later, telling the story, Hisako said:

"That morning, I had overslept a little. So, I hurriedly washed the diapers of Hiroko and Aiko, which was my daily responsibility, and put them out to dry. I remember noticing the bright blue sky as I was hanging them.

"I ran inside the house, changed into my work clothes, and grabbed my purse. I was putting on my shoes before opening the front door, when there was a powerful blast of white light, and I fainted.

"When I woke up, I saw that I was lying on my four-year-old sister Fumiko. I had unknowingly protected her, as she was near me when I fell. Without thinking, I picked her up and went out to the garden because the roof of our house had collapsed. I saw that our needle shop across from the garden was crushed. Then, I saw my mother lying under a magnolia tree that was burnt black. She was bathed in broken glass. 'Don't worry, mom. It'll be okay,' I said. I didn't know it at the time, but my bloody face didn't give my mom much hope.

"At first, she couldn't open her eyes because of the blood that was flowing into them. But helping to clear away some of the blood, she slowly opened one eye and then the other.

"Suddenly, I turned to see my brother Yutaka and sister Shizue approaching us. They had planned to stay home from school because of that morning's siren warning. They were both under the fallen roof of the house but managed to help each other escape.

"Joining us, my sister screamed out, 'There is no humanity.' And then a moment later, shouted, 'Where are Hiroko and Aiko?'

"Hiroko and Aiko had been sleeping comfortably in the mosquito net when I passed them while dressing for work. Now there was no sound of their crying. If you were alive, we would have heard their cries. But we heard nothing from our destroyed home.

"My mother figured that she'd never see her twin daughters again. From the moment I woke up from fainting, I was more concerned about the safety of these two babies than anyone else. But since our house had turned to rubble, I also thought there was no hope of the twins being saved. 'They're not alive anymore,' my mother painfully said. 'But we have to look for them.'

"My mother and I were afraid that we might be hit again by another powerful bomb. And we were also concerned about secondary disasters caused by moving collapsed roofs and broken pillars. Being early morning we weren't dressed for a survival situation. We only had on light clothes and all of us had bloody wounds. Even if we survived, we had those to contend with. But the twins were the upmost on our minds.

"However, in such a situation, it was dangerous to enter a collapsed house without shoes or gloves. We may end up losing our own lives. So, with a 'demon's heart', my mother gave up on her twin babies' lives, in favor of saving the lives of her other children.

"My father had gone out of the house, early in the morning to join the city's maintenance team. My eldest brother, Tamotsu, was on his way to the shipyard to work there. My sister Tsuneko had left for school. *What happened to them?* I

23

thought in my hazy mind. *Was it even possible that any of them could come back unharmed, let alone alive?*

"So there we were, the five of us; my mother, my two sisters, my brother and me, all huddled together in the garden, encouraging each other while waiting for more bombs to drop. We would find out later that only one special bomb was enough to turn our city into a graveyard."

The house that the Nakamura family called 'our fun home' had collapsed miserably with scattered roof tiles, broken pillars and boards, countless pieces of glass and pottery, pots, kettles, textbooks, and the children's toys. All destroyed by a single plane named after a 'courageous red-haired mother.'

5
BREAKFAST

When the Enola Gay's bomb was falling for 53 seconds, stage actress Midori Naka got up from her tatami mattress, put on a light housecoat over her panties and walked to the kitchen. Midori said:

"When it happened, I was alone in the kitchen, since it was my turn to make breakfast for the other actors. Suddenly, a white light filled the room. My first reaction was that the hot water boiler must have exploded. I immediately lost consciousness.

"When I came to, I was in darkness. Then, I gradually became aware that I was pinned beneath the ruins of the house. When I tried to work my way free, I realized that apart from my small panties, I was entirely naked as the explosion had either blow off or burnt off my housecoat. I ran my hand over my face and back: I was uninjured. Only my hands and legs were slightly scratched.

"I freed myself from the rubble on top of me and worked my way outside where I saw that everything was in flames. I ran, just as I was, to the river, jumped into the water, and floated downstream. After a few hundred yards, some soldiers fished me out."

6
SHELTER

A few minutes after detonation, five of the ten members of the Nakamura family were still in the garden. There was the family-made air-raid shelter there, but in their dazed minds, no one mentioned to enter it, even though they thought that other bombs might start falling.

Hisako said:

"After a while, we could see there was a fire approaching the neighborhood. It would eventually reach us and burn down what was left of our house, turning it to ashes. Just in case the twins, Hiroko and Aiko, were alive, I didn't want to imagine them having such a miserable death by fire. Talking it over, we five agreed to search for them. I assisted my mother who still had blood remaining in her eyes, but now could keep them open enough to see.

"Suddenly, Shizue, the quietest of our family, headed to our house. At first, I thought that she might be trying to escape the area. But she crawled into the rubble of our house in hopes to rescue Hiroko and Aiko. I followed, feeling a sudden burst of responsibility, with my mother feeling her way behind me.

"As Shizue and I pulled away fallen boards and tiles, we saw a muddy, blue mosquito net. Digging further revealed a white gauze undershirt. Pulling it away cautiously, there was one of my baby sisters lying on her stomach. It was Hiroko. Removing more ruble, we saw my baby sister Aiko. Both of their bodies were slightly stiffened, and they had their eyes closed. Shizue and I carried them out of our fallen house and into our garden.

"Seeing the twins were alive, my mother started tearing off the sleeves of the kimono she was wearing. She moistened it with water from our well and wiped Hiroko's face making her blink. I took the wet kimono sleeve from my mother and wiped Aiko's face. Her closed eyelids blinked open. I was overjoyed. The twins only had some minor scratches. It was a miracle they had survived.

"My aunt's words echoed in my mind: '*Children of good fortune.*'"

7
SHOVEL

Carrying the twins back to the garden, the five Nakamura's could see the thick atomic mushroom cloud covering the sky, darkening the whole area. "What is that?" Shizue asked.

"Something new, maybe," Hisako surmised and was right.

"What time is it?" Hisako's mother asked.

"I don't know for sure," Hisako answered. "I think It's still around 9 or 10 in the morning."

"I wonder about the others," mother Taeko said, "Your father, Tsuneko ... and ... "

Hisako, the eldest daughter, was also worried about what happened to her sister Tsuneko. She was a fifth grader at Oshiba Elementary School. She had left for school before the explosion and even though at least an hour had passed, she hadn't returned.

"There's a fire approaching," Hisako pointed out. "It's too dangerous to stay here. We have to get away. And we have to find Tsuneko."

"We should get to Kabe," Taeko said, referring to her husband's sister's house. "Tsuneko's school is on the way," she added.

The school was a mere 200 meters north of them, so they could get to her quickly. But what would they find? Would it be better to find nothing, instead of something?

Kabe is 22 kilometers from Hiroshima. At a normal walking speed of 5 kilometers an hour, it would usually take someone a little over four hours to get there. However, in the shape they were in, plus carrying the twins and stopping to rest, the journey could take twice that long.

Normally it would be a peaceful trek to get there. But now, who knew what dangers they might encounter on the way? Who could tell what people had turned into after the detonation? Also, it could be a field day for *yakuza* gangsters to prey on the weak evacuees carrying money. Prey on the fragile even more than before. But the only choice the three women had was to evacuate their destroyed home with the twins, and head for the shelter of a relative.

The five began to leave the garden, with Hisako and Shizue carrying the twins. Then mother Taeko, remembered the signal that the family agreed on when the war began: If there was an air raid and the house was destroyed, and if they were to leave the garden, they would lean a shovel against the door of the air-raid shelter. That would show anyone from the family that came to check, that at least one of them was alive and would come back home sometime.

This idea came from the last scene of the masterpiece movie *The Yellow Handkerchief of Happiness*, directed by Yoji Yamada, starring Ken Takakura, and Chieko Baisho. It can be said that it's a *'shovel filled with the love and hope for the family.'*

Taeko saw one of their many shovels lying in the garden with a blackened handle. She slowly picked it up. Seeing what she was doing, Shizue gently took the shovel from her mother's hands. "I'll do it," she said, and carefully leaned the shovel on the shelter's galvanized iron plate front door. She hoped that one or more of their missing family would be alive to come upon it when returning.

The three family members who were unaccounted for were; the father Yaichi the eldest son, Tamotsu, who went to work at the shipyard. And his sister Tsuneko, who was at her elementary school. If they had survived and saw the shovel, they would know the meaning.

Tsuneko had been in the school playground at the morning assembly during detonation. Her principal said:

"I casually looked up at the sky and saw a silver light in the distance. It was so dazzling that I held my hand above my eyes. Suddenly, my eyes saw nothing but white. The next moment my body flew into the air and I bounced on the ground like a rubber ball, with the loud explosion ringing in my ears.

Tsuneko said:

"I was standing in the middle of the school playground when suddenly I was blown all the way across to the fence. Sitting up, I looked around. The children were also blown down, crying and screaming. I looked for our teacher, but I didn't see her."

The explosion had knocked down Tsuneko. She wanted to cry like everyone else. But she was a class president and took her position seriously. She called out the names of her classmates and guided them to cover under a big willow tree next to the school gate, encouraging her classmates and the junior students.

Suddenly she heard her name being called out. Tsuneko turned to see her older sister Hisako approaching barefoot. "Hey, Hisako," Tsuneko called back. They hugged with tears in their eyes.

Being outside during the detonation, Tsuneko was severely burned all over her body. In particular, the burn on her right hand, which she had held over her eyes, seemed to be especially bad.

"Mother, Shizue, Yutaka, and I have the twins," Hisako told her. "We're going to Aunt Yoshiko's house in Kabe to get away before more bombs are dropped." She gently took Tsuneko by her less injured hand, but she wouldn't move.

"I can't run away," Tsukeno said. "I'm the class president. I have to help my friends. I have to stay until the end."

"You've been seriously burned," Hisako said. "We have to find a doctor for you."

Still, Tsuneko didn't move. Her mother Taeko and her brother and sisters approached carrying the twins. "Even if you-all try to persuade me to leave," Tsuneko insisted, "I just won't listen."

Finally, her mother, having more authority over Tsuneko than her school loyalties, ordered her to come with the family to Kabe.

As for the school, eventually, teachers and soldiers with minor burns and neighborhood people came to help. They brought the injured and immobile students into the school building that had survived without collapsing. It became an emergency evacuation site from then on.

Tsuneko's Oshiba National Elementary School was 2.4 kilometers north of *ground zero*: the point on the earth's surface directly below an exploding nuclear bomb. The wooden north school building and auditorium collapsed in an instant. Only the new school building on the south side remained. It was built strong and low so it could withstand the blast, while the other buildings collapsed instantly.

The large willow tree, where Tsuneko and her student friends gathered, endured the heat of the blast and continued to live. However, a large typhoon in 1991 caused damage to the trunk. Even so, the following year, it was transplanted near the school gate. It survives to this day with its branches and leaves ever-growing, casting a green shade over today's children in the playground.

8
EVACUATION

Taeko Nakamura knew it was urgent to get what family was with her to evacuate the area as soon as possible. Hiroshima and its surrounding areas would have no food, no place to sleep, and every hospital was in a state of devastation. So, there would be little treatment available for injuries and burns.

To make matters worse, fires had spread from the city to the surrounding areas. Waves of funeral-like processions of evacuees had already formed and was slowly moving north on the Kabe Highway.

With her husband and eldest son still missing, Taeko and her seven children set out for her sister-in-law's home in Kabe.

Kabe, currently the Asakita Ward in Hiroshima City, is a mountain town in the northern part of Hiroshima Prefecture. It's about 15 kilometers north of the Nakamura's now demolished home. It was connected to Hiroshima via the Kabe Line. But, of course, the train had stopped operating due to the catastrophe.

Kabe had suffered no damage from air raids. Nor was there any damage from the detonations of the new American bomb as it was far from *ground zero*. Walking normally, it will take more than four hours to reach Kabe. However, it was slower going for the Nakamura family carrying the twin babies, Hiroko and Aiko, now four months old. Adding to that fact is they were all suffering from wounds, bruises, and burns. Tsuneko's burns were especially bad, as she had been directly exposed to the heat of the detonation, making walking almost impossible, but she carried on as best she could.

It was past noon when rain poured on the evacuees, but it soon stopped. However, the sun remained dim due to the black clouds. The harsh, humid heat of the summer made the eight Nakamura's trek north especially daunting. But they pressed on, one foot slowly in front of the other.

The twin babies were carried by their mother and second daughter Shizue. Tsuneko walked barefoot with her severe burns. Behind them, Yutaka took Fumiko's hand, giving her encouragement that things would be better once they reached Kabe.

At the beginning of their journey, there was some slight conversation. Soon their movements and facial expressions became dull, and everyone remained silent as their forward progress proceeded at a turtle's pace.

The pain of their injuries and burns became worse as the heat and their tiredness increased. At first, Yutaka, who was in the third grade, was energetic, like he was going on a school excursion. But gradually he walked face down with heavy steps like they were walking carefully through a morgue hoping not to remain there. This was the case with all the evacuees; walking corpses exposed to the heat rays of the mysterious bomb. They walked lined up on both sides of the Kabe Highway, heading for what? Salvation? Hopefully.

The walking-wounded tried to avert their eyes from the terrible sights of the fallen that had also lined the road, on both sides and the middle. But there was no escaping the visions of horror. Some that walked, stumbled, and fell, never to get up. And yet the line of survivors kept prodding north.

Midorii is a town located on the way to Kabe. The director of the Imai Hospital was well-known in the area as a good surgeon. The image of him in Tsuneko's mind helped encouraged her to tolerate the pain of her wounds which were being attacked now and then by flies.

At one point, a truck driven by a soldier stopped. The soldier said to mother Taeko, "Hey, how far are you going?"

"We are trying to get to Midorii."

"Then please get in," the soldier said, pointing to the door on the other side of the truck.

Even with that life-saving invitation, the Nakamura's found it difficult to put their feet on the loading platform to get in. Seeing this, the soldier got out and leaned against the platform, as each of the family climbed on him as he helped them aboard by pushing each one's back.

"Thank you so much," Taeko said to him.

"We all have to help each other," the soldier said. "And we have to be patient until Japan wins the war."

Win the war against that mysterious bomb? Taeko wondered. Looking at the soldier from behind him, she could see that his clothes there were mostly burnt off and he had burns on his back.

The truck carrying the Nakamura family arrived at Imai Hospital. When each of the family members were helped off, they saw many injured people walking around trying to enter the hospital. Rescue trucks were arriving one after another with injured survivors. Some had died in the trucks.

There is a record of Hiroshima written by the director of Imai Clinic at that time.

The director said:

"The staff, including young doctors, were taken away to help soldiers in the field, so only the director of the hospital was in attendance to give treatment to the arriving injured.

"On August 6, injured people rushed in from the morning. I skipped breakfast, lunch, and supper to treat patients without sleeping all night. But I still couldn't handle it at all."

Finally, the director was exhausted with the line of patients needing treatment that got longer and longer. Even if people could get to the hospital there were no bandages or medicine to take care of them.

This was the situation when the Nakamura's arrived making it impossible to treat Tsuneko's condition. So, the family had no choice but to continue on to Kabe. Had Taeko given up hope of ever seeing her husband and eldest son Tamotsu? If she had, it remained unspoken.

With nightfall approaching, the Nakamura's reached the small village of Yagi, about five kilometers from Kabe. Passing an old-fashion teahouse, they heard a woman's voice saying, "I'm so sorry about what happened in Hiroshima. Please rest here a minute and have some tea."

They turned to see a woman as old as time beckoning them with a concerned nod of her head.

Hisako said years later:

"We sat outside next to the woman's teahouse. The woman was so old and frail that she could barely pour the tea from the pot into the cracked wooden cup that we all shared.

"When I took a sip, the warm water from my mouth to my throat felt like it was gratefully being absorbed into my body. As it finally soaked into my stomach, it felt like it was entering an empty glass jar with a popping sound.

"Being familiar with the Bible, as well as Buddhist scriptures, I thought of this old woman like the Samaritan Woman that appears in the New Testament. The one who gave Christ '*the water of life*' when he was resting from traveling.

"To us, it was the '*tea of life*' for sure. It felt like the first time drinking that delicious barley tea. I felt reborn. We all bowed our heads, thanking our newfound *spiritual grandmother* for her concern, her sharing and giving us heart to continue. 'Please be careful on your journey', she said as we slowly departed her small teahouse. 'Remember,' she added, 'You are in control of your fate.'

"As we slowly walked away, we kept looking back at the teahouse, giving a wave to that wonderful woman, who gave a slow wave back every time. Finally, when we looked back, the teahouse and the woman had disappeared in the darkness and distance."

Years later, Taeko remembered the truck soldier and the teahouse grandmother's kindness. She said, "I knew at that time that, even if we were to lose the war, the Japanese people would not die, and that our family would surely survive."

9
KABE

The eight Nakamura family members arrived in Kabe in the dead of night. Surrounded by mountains, the town had a feeling of protection for the group. Yaichi's sister's house was small but sturdy. A river was flowing close by, making the atmosphere sound and feel fresh and natural. Quite a contrast from the last twelve hours. Hisako remembered the situation well.

Hisako said:

"We were greeted warmly by Aunt Yoshiko and Uncle Daimon, who immediately comforted us with food, clothes, and attention. 'Stay here as long as necessary,' my aunt said with my uncle encouraging us to feel at ease in their home.

"When we asked about our two teenage cousins, we were alarmed to hear that their daughters had gone to Hiroshima early in the morning and hadn't returned yet. Though we didn't say it, we all feared that they had unluckily been victims of the bomb.

"Uncle Daimon wept in front of the altar saying, 'On the way out, leaving for Hiroshima, our daughters said, 'We want to eat soybeans there.' They wanted soybeans, and now … perhaps they are gone.'

"The terrible irony struck me; although we lived in Hiroshima, we were saved. But my two cousins lived here safely surrounded by mountains, yet they picked that day to decide to eat soybeans in Hiroshima. However, it was not known at that time if the girls had been killed or not."

"Don't worry," Taeko encouraged her sister and brother-in-law. "I'm sure they'll be back soon."

However, Daimon could not be consoled. He remained at the alter while his wife showed the family where they could wash up and sleep.

Hisako said:

"When I washed my head with fresh water, my fingers could not get between my hair because it was caked with dust, blood, and sweat. There was no shampoo at that time. Even soap was a valuable item then. So I continued to let the water do the best it could. My hair was still not perfectly clean when I finally laid down on a cool tatami mat, but I felt much better, and quickly slept."

Taeko spent the night hugging her twins on the veranda, looking up at the dark sky wondering about her husband Yaichi and her eldest son Tamotsu.

10
YAICHI

The head of the Nakamura household, Yaichi, was supposed to go to the road expansion construction site on the morning of the detonation. It was about a ten-minute bicycle ride from his house to the site.

Yaichi said:

"I left home a little earlier than usual that day, so I decided to stop by a friend's house on the way. He invited me in to have some tea. I parked by bicycle and entered his house. He poured the tea, and as I brought the cup up to my mouth I said, 'It's going to get hot today.' Right then, there was a flash of light. My friend's home was about one kilometer from where the bomb hit, so when the light struck me, I instantly went unconscious.

"When I woke up, I was under the house, and I couldn't move. I shouted out for help, but I didn't hear any reply. Not my friend nor his family answered back.

"Soon, I realized that a fire had started. Then came yellow smoke swirling around me. I used all my strength to break a piece of wood that was covering me. I realized that I was partially in the fireplace. It was the bricks of that fireplace that had miraculously saved my life.

"I went outside and could see there was rubble everywhere. The city that I was so familiar with had disappeared from sight. There were flames and black smoke rising out of where the city used to stand. Around the area there were injured people, crying in agony.

"My first thought was for my family. I quickly looked for my bicycle but didn't see it. So I headed home on foot. Suddenly, it began to rain, and I could see some of the fires weaken. But when the rain stopped just as suddenly, the fires regained their power.

"It was so hot that I jumped into the nearby river to cool off, and then continued to my home. Along the riverbank, I saw people falling into the river and being swept away like sticks. Something I'd like to forget ... but can't.

"When I finally arrive home, I was shocked to see that my house had been flattened. Could anyone in my family have survived that? Probably not, I feared. Both the pine trees next to my house had been charred black. I thought, *if the blast from that white light could do that to my trees, what did it do to my family?*

"As I looked around my house feeling miserable, I saw our air-raid shelter. There was something like a burnt stick leaning against the entrance. I focused on it and realized it wasn't a stick. It was a shovel. Could it be our arranged signal? Was one or more of my family alive? Or had the shovel been blasted over there?

"I hurriedly peeled off the galvanized iron plate that had closed the shelter's entrance and went inside. But no one was there. Since both the house and the garden were burnt, they must have evacuated somewhere because of the danger. That meant someone might come back soon. A little light of hope came to me.

"I figured that I should wait here until someone returned. I was a little relieved, but so tired and painful that I laid down in the shelter.

"In a few minutes, I heard someone's voice. I jumped up and looked out of the shelter. I saw a dark shadow standing by the house. 'Who is it?' I called out. The shadow didn't speak but waved to me slowly as it approached."

"Father?" his eldest son asked.

"Tamotsu? I can't believe it."

The 17-year-old Tamotsu approached, and they carefully hugged each other. Stepping back, they both pointed at each other giving a slight smile and chuckle. Each saw the other's face black with soot, dust, blood, and tears. Tamotsu's face had something extra: coal tar.

11
TAMOTSU

Tamotsu Nakamura was thought to be the most handsome boy in his school. He was often compared to Tyrone Power, as the Japanese were familiar with the American actor by such movies as: *The Mark of Zorro, Jesse James,* and *Blood and Sand.*

When walking the halls of his high school, Tamotsu would often see girls, in twos and threes, sneaking looks at him, whispering and giggling. It was a challenge for a teenage boy to survive that daily. However, it was summer break, so there were no giggly girls to contend with where he worked at the docks to earn extra money for the family.

Tamotsu said:

"I went to the Mitsubishi Shipyard that morning with other young workers. That day, I was assigned to work inside the bottom of the ship. Suddenly, there was a loud noise that shook us violently. The ship was rocking so much that I wondered if it was an earthquake, tidal wave, or a direct hit from a B-29. Whatever it was, I knew it was dangerous to be there, so I came topside with the others and looked out from the deck of the ship toward the land.

"I was astonished to see that the usual scenery that should be there, that was always there, had disappeared. There were no trains or buses. It was like being *spirited away*. There were shadows of people rolling around as if they had been thrown around like burnt leaves in a wind. When I arrived in the morning, everything had been fine. But now it was dark, like a city of death.

"When I got control of my astonishment, my first thought was my family at home. Could they still be here on earth? Or were they also thrown around like leaves?

"It was about 3 kilometers to my house. The road was abnormally burnt and hot with my *jikatabi* work shoes providing little protection. Soon my feet were burning hot. But I put up with it as I desperately wanted to get home.

"Looking up, I saw that there were no enemy planes in the sky, so it seemed that there would be no second or third wave bombing. However, it was strange indeed to see that everything was burnt no matter where I looked or how far I walked. I saw a blackened concrete building with the windows blown out. I saw trees that were still standing, but their trunks and branches were dark with the leave blown off. There were fires rising up most places I looked.

"How could a single explosion, a single bomb cause so much widespread damage? Was I having a bad dream? I actually pinched my cheeks. It was painful, but proved that this was no dream that I was walking in.

"I finally arrived at our house. I was totally disheartened to see that it was completely destroyed with fires burning in various places. However, I could see that our air-raid shelter was still intact with a shovel leaning on it. 'Is there anyone there?' I called out. There was no reply, but in a few moments, I saw movement at the shelter door. It was body-language more than his blackened face that told me it was my father.

"After hugging, I asked him the obvious question, but he had no idea about how many of our family survived or when whoever left the shovel would return. We spent the night in the shelter. In the middle of the night, I momentarily stepped out of the shelter and looked up at the sky. There were no stars. The single bomb had erased them, too."

12
WATER

The small mountain town of Kabe was full of displaced people from Hiroshima. The injured were housed in temples and schools. The police station was also crowded with seriously injured survivors.

The morning after arriving in Kabe, Hisako carried Tsuneko on her back to the police station to treat her burns. Their grandfather went with them to be sure they would be helped. However, there was no doctor nor medicine there, just oil. Still, Tsuneko felt a slight relief and was grateful for it.

On the way out of the hospital, an old man said, "I know a natural remedy. Burn some *leopard plant* leaves and make a lotion for your burns."

The *leopard plant* is a perennial that grows in the shade. Its leaves and stems have a strong antibacterial effect that has been used as folk medicine. It's very effective for healing wounds and burns.

The next day, Hisako burned the leaves and mixed it into a salve. She gave it to Tsuneko who gently applied it to her wounds.

Tsuneko said:

"Uncle Daimon gave me a clean mixing stick from the kitchen to treat myself with the mixture. I very gently rubbed it on my wounds. Right away, pus began to spill out. Every time that happened, that area on my skin felt much better."

Shizue, the second daughter, who was less injured than the others, went to a Zen temple in the town to help care for the injured.

Shizue said:

"Even with the horrible situation that was happening at the temple, I worked there day and night to do what I could to help. I remember one injured man at the temple who was crying out, 'Please give me water.' I could hardly tell where his mouth was because of his swollen face. I went to get a cup of water, even though, for some reason I didn't understand, I was told not to give water to him. I let him drink it knowing that it would soon turn into *terminal water*, as he was destined to be carried to the riverbank with the rest of the deceased.

"Even though I know that would happen, I felt that I had to be kind to him. I couldn't ignore his urgent cry for water. Even if he didn't get water, I knew he would pass away after a few hours. Wasn't he a little happier to drink water and die with some satisfaction, than to die with the pain of thirst on top of his other pains?

"The answer was obvious to me at that time. And even now, I think I made the right choice."

13
MIRACLE

When Taeko was breastfeeding the twins, Hiroko and Aiko, they seemed to never be satisfied. They cried all the time. Now Taeko was cradling them in her arms to sooth them when she heard the front door open. She went to the foyer to greet Uncle Daimon, but instead, she saw a man with a dusty, blackened face. A face that for some strange reason smiled with tired pride, showing white teeth.

"It's me," the man proclaimed proudly. And proud he should be. He had survived Hiroshima and made the trip to Kabe safely. It was Yaichi, her husband.

Holding her twin babies in her arms while looking at her given-up-for-dead husband, Taeko stood mute. Only her tears showed Yaichi her happiness to see him. He approached, and ever so gently embraced his wife and babies.

"Are you alone?" the words finally came to Taeko.

"Yes," Yaichi said, but quickly added. "Tamotsu is okay. Thanks to God, he was deep in the ship he was working on when the explosion came."

"Then where is he?" she asked.

"I left him back at our air-raid shelter."

"Then it's a miracle," she wept. "All ten of us survived. We were all two kilometers from where the bomb hit and we're alive."

Then Uncle Diamon entered the room. "Yachi-san. You're alive. Thank, God."

"Yes, I made it. We all made it."

"I'm also glad that you can take care of your family here," Uncle Diamon said. "I have to leave and search for my daughters in Hiroshima."

"In Hiroshima?" Yaichi said. "I'm so sorry. Yes, of course you must go. But how will you get there?"

"I'll go by bicycle."

"I understand that you must go," Yaichi said. "But I have to tell you, it's a terrible road. You'll see horrible things."

"I'm afraid so. But I'll just keep my head down and peddle. I should get there in about an hour."

"It'll take you longer than that the way the roads are jammed with people … alive or not."

"Well, I'll just do my best."

"If you don't find them by nightfall, I hope you'll return here."

"I'll see what happens," Uncle Daimon said, leaving the house.

"Take care," Yaichi said.

Yaichi went into the small living room and sat down on the cool tatami mat. It had been a tremendously long day for all. Yet, it was actually three days all jammed into the feeling of one terrible day.

Taeko set the babies down next to Yaichi and went into the garden. She looked up at the sky and mountains, then closing her eyes, she put her hands together and said a prayer of gratitude to her ancestors. Surely, they were watching and had blessed her and her family during this trial of body and spirit.

Taeko said:

"It was at that moment that I received a revelation about my great grandfather, Kichizaemon Wada. Since he was a child, he believed that his father came down from heaven and sat in front of him. I could now feel the power of my spiritual ancestors aiding me and all the surviving families who had endured this catastrophe.

"From the end of the Edo period to the turbulent times of the Meiji era, my great grandfather gave his private fortune to his clan. He was thought of as a guardian deity who protected families who were having difficult times. There, in my husband's sister's garden, on that day, I gathered strength from my great grandfather's spirit. I closed my eyes and prayed.

"After a while, I opened my eyes. In the distance I could see a dark towering cloud rising up at the edge of the distant blue mountains. The cloud looked like a human being with legs crossed. When I squinted, I thought it looked exactly like the statue of great grandfather Wada that I saw when I was a child. 'Thank you, grandfather,' I said quietly.

"After talking to my family about this revelation, we decided when these dangerous times were behind us, we would visit the Wada family gravesite in their hometown of Otake City.

What kind of person was the great grandfather of mother Taeko, Wada? What kind of person was Kichizaemon Wada?

PART TWO

HUMANITARIAN

A person seeking to promote human welfare.

14
KARMA

Mother Taeko Nakamura was born into the Wada family in 1904. She grew up in Ogata Village in the Hiroshima prefecture. The Wada family served as soy sauce brewers in their village for generations, since the Edo era.

Taeko's grandfather, Kichizaemon, had the family brewery handed down to him at the young age of 18. Even though the times were turbulent, he made great achievements in the development of his local community.

The stone monument that was erected in Kichizaemon's honor is still maintained by the Otake City as a historic site, along with the Wada family building. To this day, many of the great achievements of Kichizaemon Wada are summarized as supplementary teaching materials for schools and used as moral lessons.

Taeko grew up listening to the humanity and achievements of her great grandfather from her parents and relatives. Every time there was good news for his family and relatives, she made prayers of thanks to Kichizaemon at the family Buddhist altar. She thought about Kichizaemon every day and grew up feeling she was watched over by him.

Taeko said:

"I thanked my ancestors when I got married, had children, and every time they went off to school or got a job. In my heart, there was always the image of Kichizaemon, like the sun."

Taeko's children grew up listening to various stories of Kichizaemon's accomplishments. In this way, the Nakamura family members lived their daily lives with the feeling of being protected by the '*barrier of goodness*' made by their powerful ancestor.

In Buddhist teachings, *human destiny* is divided into good and evil, depending on the actions of individuals: bad rewards for bad deeds and good rewards for good deeds. The law of cause and effects; *karma*. This *karma* is handed down to the ancestors of that person. Thus, the family believed that they inherited the good karma from the good deeds of Kichizaemon.

Concerning the unprecedented disaster of Hiroshima, all ten of the Nakamura family were able to survive. Taeko believed that it was the culmination of the good deeds of her grandfather that brought about her family's salvation.

Later that night after Yaichi's return, the family knelt down facing the direction of Kichizaemon's village of Ogata. They held hands, lowered their heads, and gave thanks for the good karma that had been passed down to them.

15
KICHIZAEMON

The Nakamuras had more challenges ahead of them. But now that they have been mostly reunited, (Tamotsu is still at the shelter in Hiroshima), let's leave them at peace momentarily and examine, in more detail, Kichizaemon Wada, the man that Taeko idolizes so much.

He was born in Ogata-mura, Saeki-gun (now Otake City, Hiroshima prefecture). At that time, it was a land rich in nature, blessed with the sea, mountains, and rivers.

He was a brilliant child and loved by everyone in the village and known as a kind-hearted boy.

At age 18, his father died so he took over the running of the family soy sauce brewing and became the *Shoya*, a kind of mayor, to the village.

Nine years later (1845), when Kichizaemon was 27, Ogata Village was hit by a great flood. Many of the houses were washed away, killing 250 people. The fields were severely damaged so crops could not be grown.

Since it was a poor village, there were no reserves. It was inevitable that starvation would occur, making some farmers sell their daughters.

It was the duty of *Shoya* to maintain a peaceful life for the villagers. Kichizaemon, who had a strong sense of responsibility, pondered what to do. He went to nearby villages and listened to their leaders' ideas.

The breakthrough that came from that was called the *Polder Project*. In front of Ogata Village was the *Seto* Inland Sea. When Kichizaemon was a child, he went to the shallow area to play, chasing small fish and picking up shellfish. Now he thought of those shallows as ideal for reclamation. If the vast land was developed as agricultural land and distributed to farmers who did not have fields, the risk of famine would be reduced. But where would the money come from to accomplish this?

Kichizaemon used the Wada family land that had been accumulated for generations as collateral and borrowed the money to pay for reclamation work.

More than 1,000 people, mainly the villagers of Ogata Village, participated in the reclamation work. The villagers worked hard building an embankment. Amazingly, they finished the task in less than a year. They cut off shallow parts of the sea, drained the water, and turned it into dry, agricultural land.

Kichizaemon wrote:

"When we were about to move on to the draining process, a fierce typhoon struck our town. The sea was swirling strongly in opposite directions. That night, all of us in the village heard a loud *bang* that startled us. It was a large wave that hit the embankment that was just on the verge of completion. We all had an uneasy night.

"I couldn't sleep at all. I had no choice but to pray to God, hoping that the typhoon would pass quickly, and that the embankment would remain intact.

"Eventually the storm subsided in the middle of the night. The villagers and I gathered on the pitch-black beach while it was still raining, though thankfully much lighter. We lit a bonfire and waited for the dawn as the sea seemed to be calming.

"In the red light of dawn, I looked out toward the sea holding my breath. Finally, I could see a black shadow just barely visible. It was the embankment. 'It's safe,' I called out to everyone.

"Cheers went up all around me. But as it grew lighter our cheers turned into disappointing sighs. Only a part of the embankment seemed to be safe. Most of it was destroyed by the rough seas."

"The dreams of my fellow villagers to own the new farmland disappeared with the disappearance of the embankment. I watched the various reactions as all our hard work had been in vain. Some just stood on the beach motionless and stared at what remained of our one year of hard work. Others knelt in prayer. Some shook their fists at the sea. Some cried. As for me, that was the worst feeling of frustration and despair I've ever felt in my life."

However, Kichizaemon was not a man to quit at anything. He believed *if you have money, you can take action on anything*. So, he re-mortgaged his land and mansion, borrowed 300 new building stones, and resumed construction. The villagers also worked harder than ever, responding to Kichizaemon 's strong willpower.

Finally, in 1851, more than 15 new parcels of land were created capable of growing crops. These lands went to the villagers to farm.

The old document recording the cost of the land reclamation is written up as *murauke*, meaning money borrowed by the village. But in reality, it was Kichizaemon who poured all his personal fortune into the project. He owed a huge amount of money because of it. He finally paid off the debt 20 years later when times became more prosperous.

16
SHIPS

When the reclamation work was completed after six years, Kichizaemon Wada was 34 years old. Because of his accomplishments and invincible spirit, he was appointed *karishoya* (town mayor) in 1853.

That year, Admiral Perry of the United States Navy arrived in four ships, now famously called *black ships*, at Tokyo harbor. Their mission was to force Japan to trade goods with America. They also demanded a treaty to open all Japanese ports to U.S. merchant ships. That would set off turbulent times in Japan.

In that era, Kichizaemon was busy as the head of the soy sauce enterprises in all his neighboring 21 villages. His main task was to collect and manage the annual taxes and to oversee the various community supervisors.

It was customary at that time to have a *warishoya,* the highest-ranking role for farmers, be one of the village elders in his late 50s, but Kichizaemon was only 35. It was the wishes of most of the villagers to have him in that position because they knew his reputation for overcoming challenges and managing people.

Kichizaemon continued to devote his life to the developing the community and the happiness of the people living there. Two years after his death at age 67, the people erected a memorial monument in appreciation for his tremendous love of humanity.

PART THREE

AFTERMATH

The consequences of a significant unpleasant event.

17
INTRUDERS

It was two days after detonation. Yaichi thought it best to take most of his family back home where the eldest son Tomatsu was waiting. Since Tsuneko was badly burned, he decided she should stay, as well as the eldest daughter Hisako, to attend to her. It seemed that the *leopard plant* leaves on Tsuneko's burns was effective. So for the time being, it was best for her to rest at his house.

Hisako said:

"I knew it was best to stay and help nurse my sister, but it wasn't a warm situation. In my Uncle Daimon's house, the eldest daughter had to prepare the daily food. With such a large family, I didn't want to be in that situation forever. But I didn't say anything. I just hoped my sister would recover enough to be comfortable enough to make the journey back to our home, for her sake and mine. But though it was 'our home', there certainly was no house remaining. What would be the situation when we returned? And what would the city and the people there be like from now on?"

"Also, there was no feeling of warmth in Uncle Daimon's house. His two daughters had gone to Hiroshima the day the bomb was dropped and there was no word from them. No returning girls to make a happy reunion as it had been when my father arrived.

"Every day, Uncle Daimon rode his bike the hour to Hiroshima in search of his daughters. Every night he returned alone with a heavy heart."

Yaichi left Daimon's house early the next morning with Taeko, Shizue, Yutaka, Fumiko and the twins, Hiroko, and Aiko. It was a slow walk with many rests and many horrible sights that they tried to avert their eyes from, but usually failed. At their slow pace it took them five hours to cover the 22 kilometers to their home. Yes, they had not dreamed it. Their house was collapsed with the remains half-burnt.

Though crestfallen from the sight of it, the sight of the eldest son Tamotsu appearing at the entrance of the shelter appearing healthy lifted their spirits.

"Since yesterday, this shelter has been our new home," Tamotsu said, waving with a slight smile.

The group was too tired to return the smile, but Yaichi managed a nod of his head to him. When they entered the shelter, they saw that Tamotsu had collected the rice and wheat straw that had not been burned. He also put in futons and kimonos that remained intact from their home, making the shelter surprisingly comfortable under the circumstances.

The next day, the family had no time to feel sad about the destruction of their home because, under the command of father Yaichi, survival work began. Temporary housing had to be built and the garden needed preparation to grow food again.

Father and son began cleaning up the wreckage of the half-burnt, collapsed house. They collected the unburned pillars, boards, and tatami mats, separating them into the usable and unusable, so they could build the temporary house.

The 9-year-old son, Yutaka, helped carry the pillars and usable nails and put them in a stack. Their well had not been damaged, so there was plenty of fresh water. Yutaka also gathered needed household items such as burnt futons, chipped bowls, and knives with soot on them. The kettle to make hot water for the bath was damaged, but that could be repaired and used.

For the time being, they had some rice and salt stored in the shelter, so that was used to make porridge. Occasionally, rice balls were distributed by concerned people from towns and villages that were less affected by the bomb.

With the material at hand, they proceeded with the construction of the temporary home. Although it was full of gaps, they didn't mind, and proceeded at a quick pace.

The preparation of the garden progressed as well. Pieces of wood and garbage were piled up to be burnt for ash that they scattered around as fertilizer.

Taeko received some vegetable seeds from a kind neighboring farmer and planted them. In a few days, the new house was finished, and the family moved from the shelter to it, grateful for at least a structure that was larger than the shelter. And it was strong enough to withstand the rain downpours that would come in droves during the August rainy season.

In a few days, the *Kabe Line* connecting Yokogawa Station with the Kabe Station was reopened, so Hisako and Tsuneko, who had been staying at their uncle's house, rode it to return to their family.

That night, Uncle Diamon and his wife were awakened by the slam of the front door and the sound of bare feet on the wood floor of the hallway. Diamon was the first to enter the hall to defend his home from possible intruders. Perhaps Hiroshima survivors searching for food and shelter. His wife quickly entered behind him with much fear for the safety of their home.

They saw, standing there in the darkness, covered in dirt, their two *given up for dead* daughters. Wherever they had been in Hiroshima, whatever road they had taken home, they would explain later. That only thing that mattered was that the two girls stood before their parents … healthy.

18
PUMPKIN

Fortunately, Tsuneko's burns had rapidly improved because of the *leopard plant* concoction that Daimon prepared for her daily. With their arrival in Hiroshima, all ten members of the Nakamura family were together again.

Hisako said:

"Because we were reunited, though the temporary housing was small and full of holes, some fun and laughter slowly returned to our home. However, we all had to work very hard to survive in our little part of Hiroshima with our burnt field.

"Naturally, there was a large food shortage in the area. Everyone was hungry and we ate whatever we could find. I caught and ate waterside frogs and field locusts. Though it doesn't sound so tasty now, at that time they were treats to me.

"I remember finding a half-burnt pumpkin in a nearby field. I picked it up, took it home and boiled it. We were all happily about it because it was the first solid food we had eaten in a long time. We loved that pumpkin ... until we didn't.

"A few hours later, we all got very sick and realized that all the local pumpkins had been exposed to radiation from the bomb and were not edible. I remembered that years later, whenever I'd see a grinning Halloween pumpkin and think, *Yeah, sure, grin you evil pumpkin. You're happy to have made us all sick*."

Yaichi, carved a Y-shaped tree-branch, attached a rubber string to it, and made a slingshot to shoot frogs and insects to eat. He also shot down sparrows and took them home. His wife Taeko peeled the wings off, baked it, and made a stew out of it. "It smelled better than it tasted," Hisako said, "But it was still a treat for us."

Near the end of the war, unused hand grenades were left scattered around where the armies used to be. Yaichi and Tamotsu, took them to the river, pulled the pins and tossed them in the water. The explosion killed crucian carp and loach catfish to fill Taeko's frying pan. Fishing with explosives is now forbidden, but at the time there was no law against it. "Even if there were a law forbidding *hand grenade fishing*," Yaichi said, years later, "we still would have done it."

19
PINEAPPLE

Yutaka Nakamura's Elementary School was being rebuilt in October. Until its completion they started holding a *Blue-Sky* classroom which was desks and pieces of blackboards linked up in the playground. Because the supply of pencils and textbooks were limited, pencils and textbooks had to be shared among the students. Yutaka's study group of eight, shared one textbook. All were happy to study diligently.

Yutaka said:

"At that time, I was always hungry. One time, in the corner of my school garden I found a round, white radish. I couldn't believe it was there. My eyes must have shined, but I know for sure that my stomach screamed 'eat it now.'

"However, I thought it would be more delicious if I took it home to have mom prepare it and eat it with my family. When I started to pull it out, it felt a little different than I expected. When I examined it closely, I realized that it was a bone, maybe one of my classmates. I tossed it away quickly, turning and running at the same time. I never went back to that area of our school."

"It turned out that our school was not safe from seeing the effects of the bomb disaster because it had become a refugee shelter. Victims flooded in, many never to return to their homes or loved ones again.

"I was so hungry one time, that I even tried eating toothpaste. But I quickly spit it out. But I do remember one tasty experience. There was a team of workers in charge of organizing the rubble of Hiroshima Castle. I went by there one day and saw some box-lunches laying around. I grabbed one of them and ate what was inside. I didn't know what it was, but the taste was so good. A long time later, I experienced that taste again. I turned out it was corned beef. I'll never forget the first time I tasted that processed meat.

"Months later, the war ended, and our school building was restored to almost its original state. I remember there were frequent supplies of food from the US miliary to our school. One thing I really liked was their canned pineapple from America. However, it was just the juice without any of the fruit part.

"Then one day, I saw the janitor of our school holding a bucket as he rode his bicycle on the way home. There was newspaper on top of the bucket, but a sudden wind blew it away. I looked inside as he passed me and was surprised to see golden pineapple fruit.

"Come to find out later, the teachers and the janitor had secretly taken the fruit parts for themselves, leaving us hungry children only the juice. I guess you could say they were bad to do that, but that was the way things were during those tough years."

20
BARTER

The US military distributed rice, sugar, flour, and other goods to Japanese families. But it was not enough to satisfy the hunger of the Nakamura family's ten members. So, mother Taeko packed her unburned kimono with what goods they had and vegetables from their garden, got on the crowded train, and went around to farmhouses to barter for needed food.

She devised a plan to save a small amount of sugar that was rationed to her, store it, then use that for bartering. The farmers were used to bartering kimonos and *kimono*-belts in exchange for their food. In the past, the farmers always had the upper hand when it came to negotiating items. But now they had to learn a new system of value for the goods they needed. Since sugar was a hard-to-get item, people were pleased with whatever they could get their hands on.

Arriving at a farm, Taeko would take out the sugar from her kimono backpack and say to the farmer, "I've got this sugar to trade."

The farmer would be immediately interested and say, "Stay right here. I have potatoes in the field. I'll trade those for your sugar."

Even though she was in the power position with her sugar, Taeko would politely bow her head, put some potatoes in her backpack, and take them home.

That was Taeko's routine in those days after the war. She would leave her house in the early morning and return with a backpack full of food. She would be bent over from the long walk, standing in the train, and carrying the load.

The twin babies, Hiroko and Aiko were around age two then, so they didn't understand what was happening to the Japanese at that time. They would just happily greet their mother on her late afternoon return.

Taeko would often have dumplings for them. Hiroko would comically eat out the middle rice and throw away the wheat skin.

Before long, a *black market* began to set up around the Yokogawa Train Station. Various unusual and suspicious things were lined up there and sold without trouble from the law … for a time. Yaichi would buy things like brown sugar and gunpowder there.

Yaichi, made dumplings from sweet potatoes from the family garden. He had his second daughter, Shizue, take them to the train station to sell. The potatoes contained very little sugar, so they weren't so sweet, but they sold like crazy. Yutaka, the glutton of the family, would eat as much as he could get his hands on and then suffer from stomach pains. The family had to continually warn him about overeating.

However, the black market was against the law, hence the word *black*. It was soon be discovered by the police and shut down, making things tougher on the Nakamura family to survive.

21
RECOVERY

The weather changed with the seasons as a year had passed since detonation. Hiroshima residents thought that grass would not grow due to the effects of radioactivity. However, eight months later, in the spring, yellow *rapeseed* blossoms began blooming in the corners of farmlands. Also, the seeds that mother Taeko had sown in the family garden were growing. The earth was steadily recovering from the Enola Gay's wrath.

The garden on the Nakamura's land was cultivated and turned into a field for farming. Each family member had their own hoe, planted, and harvested vegetables. There were many delicious vegetables such as sweet potatoes, radishes, and pumpkins … non-radioactive thankfully.

The variety of food on the table steadily increased. Even flowers were added to their temporary house. As the earth recovered from the *awakened giant,* who was now helping in Japan's recovery, the family recovered.

The family's temporary home expanded slightly, giving everyone more elbow room. The kitchen and bath were put under a new tin roof in a separate, small building. In the summer, when bathing, the family could see the moon though gaps in the tin roof and hear the sound of insects.

At that time, many houses didn't have a bath, so a man in the neighborhood said to Yaichi, "You know, even after your large family takes a bath, the water is still hot, so I was wondering if you'd let me take a bath sometime after your family is finished?" Yaichi said it would be okay. That was the kind comradery there was amongst the city's survivors.

The second daughter, Shizue, took care of the twins who were now three years old. One time, she took the twins out for a walk and passed a church.

Shizue said:

"At the front of the church, there was an American soldier working on repairs. He motioned to us, and when we came closer, he gave all three of us pieces of chocolate. After that, I took the twins by the church almost every day to get more. Sometimes he gave us biscuits and chewing gum.

"My mother worked hard from the early morning, doing the housework for the ten of us and raising the twins. I helped by starting the fire in the stove every morning and preparing box lunches for the children that went to school, and for Hisako who worked at the *Shinkin* Credit Union.

"Of course, there were no washing machines, so all our clothes were handwashed on a washboard. After drying the laundry we did our field work and weeding. At nightfall, we started preparing dinner. With the little food we had, we made sure that the children ate well so they didn't get sick. At night, we had sewing work to do, such as repairing the torn clothes of our playful children."

22
PIKADON

Two months after detonation, October 14, 1945, among the first U.S sailors to come ashore at Hiroshima was the renowned society piano player Eddy Duchin. He would later be made more famous in the movie *The Eddy Duchin Story* starring Tyrone Power.

Duchin and some sailors entered what remained of a hospital where survivors lay motionless. Wandering into an open solarium room filled with broken glass, they saw a piano still in playable condition.

Francis Lestingi, a sailor who was there, said:

"Eddy Duchin sat down and began playing his inimitable rendition of *Tea for Two*. I'll never forget how the eyes of those patients began to move and their heads started turning toward the direction the music was coming from. It seemed as though life was arising."

Indeed, two years after detonation, the daily lives of the Hiroshima survivors slowly and steadily began to recover. Mother Taeko said, "Each dawn, a better morning seemed to come into my house."

However, the positive feeling of the morning light was to the Nakamura family, they, and others of Hiroshima, could feel that something was gaining on them. Namely, the lingering dark shadow of that single blast that had whited out so many.

The scars on people's skin and the fears of what the long-term effects of atomic radiation might bring, remained in the survivor's minds. The fear of *pikadon poison*.

Those witnessing the Hiroshima detonation coined the term *Pikadon*, meaning *flash-boom* in Japanese. First the blinding light, then a deafening explosion. Later came the term: *pikadon poison*, the effects of atomic radiation.

That aftermath fear had never left father Yaichi's mind. And one day, in the second year after the detonation, his fear manifested itself. Would it bring down the Nakamura family's pillar of strength?

First, Yaichi felt the taste of blood in his mouth. Testing with his finger, he saw that indeed it was blood. He thought nothing of it … at first.

Years later Yaichi said:

"What is this? I thought. Is my hair going to start falling out next? I started thinking, *'Is this pikadon poisoning come to eat me?'* At that time, even two years later, information about the atomic bomb nor radiation poisoning had not been released by the government.

88

"There was only hearsay amongst the residents about what the effects might be. I remembered the day of the bomb and how I had walked back to my home in the black rain. I was the only one who survived from the local labor force, because of my inadvertent tea break on the way to work. But now? Was it my turn?"

The bleeding of Yaichi's gums continued, followed by hair loss and purple spots appearing on his skin. Next came a high fever that continued for days. From what he had heard, Yaichi knew this was a typical reaction to radiation-induced symptoms.

To the possible rescue of Yaichi and other radiation victims came: Dr. Masato Tsutsumi, Vice Chairman of the *Acupuncture and Moxibustion Society of Saeki-gun* in the Hiroshima Prefecture. He was treating numerous victims of the Enola Gay. The results of his experiments on a *'large number of patients'* supposedly resulted in *'miraculous recoveries'*.

Of the dozens of patients that Dr. Tsutsumi had, three had been completely cured. Four of them were not completely cured. The remaining were said to be 'improving'. Also, five of the seriously injured people with high fevers, burns, hair loss and skin spots were said to 'all be improving.'

Dr. Tsutsumi used *moxibustion,* also called *moxa treatment.* This was derived from traditional Chinese medicine that came to Japan as well as other Asian countries. It is performed by burning small cones of dried leaves on special *acupuncture* points on the body.

The term *moxibustion* comes from the name of the *wormwood* plant that is commonly used in the treatment. The doctor proved that it had the effect of preventing the destruction of white and red blood cells, and then increasing them to return the patient to health.

The doctor was known to have been the doctor in charge of the actress Midori Naka. After she had been rescued from the river in Hiroshima, four days later, on the morning of August 10, she was put on the first train to Tokyo.

On August 16, she was admitted to the University of Tokyo Hospital where, despite Dr. Tsusumi's attention, her condition deteriorated rapidly, passing away six days later.

"She could not help but love drama," remembered Seiji Ikeda, another actor who had performed with her. "She was far from beautiful, but she had a big heart. She was like a big sister to those around her."

Midori was the first person in the world whose death was officially certified to be a result of *atomic bomb disease* (radiation poisoning). The publicity surrounding the illness of Midori, owing to her status as a public figure, was instrumental in catapulting the so-called *radiation sickness* to the public eye.

Under the leadership of Dr. Masao Tsuzuki, head of the *Japanese National Research Council*, much critical clinical data was collected in the first month after detonation. Their studies were invaluable but were largely suppressed from publication by the occupying US military. This was because Dr. Tsuzuki had the rank of rear admiral in the Japanese Navy.

Both the Japanese and American military had an inclination for secrecy. Still, he became known as *the father of atomic bomb research.*

It is not known, if Taeko Nakamura heard about Dr. Tsuzuki's moxibustion treatment of the *bomb disease* from publications or word of mouth, but she totally believed in the cure. When she realized the illness had come to her husband Yaichi, she presented him with the information.

"I won't do it," Yaichi responded to his wife. "I'll heal naturally step by step. I'll just put up with the discomfort."

Indeed, at that time, many wondered if the *moxibustion treatment* really worked. But there was much talk of cures by this method.

Yaichi said:

"When I was working in the field, a U.S Army Jeep stopped, and I was taken to a hospital. They tested my blood and checked various parts of my body, and then took X-rays. I thought that the doctors would diagnose and treat my condition on my next visit, but they never set an appointment. That was all they wanted with me. So I figured that to them I was just a human guinea pig."

It is a fact that the role of the *Atomic Bomb Casualty Commission* was not to provide treatment, but to collect data in preparation for other possible nuclear wars by the U.S. military. All the examination data collected in Japan was sent to U.S. military agencies. So it was a military institution with a completely different purpose than medical treatment for survivors of the atomic bomb. Japanese doctors and nurses were involved in the study, and the A-bomb survivors were only used to gather the information. Indeed, *guinea pigs*.

Finally, after days of encouragement, both gentle and forceful, from his wife Taeko, Yaichi agree to try the treatment from a local doctor. The small, hot pyramid cones were placed on as many acupoints of Yaichi's body as possible. He had the treatment once or twice every day.

At the same time, Taeko clung to the blessings of her grandfather Wada and prayed for Yaichi's recovery at the family Buddhist altar every morning and night.

After three months, of treatment and devoted nursing from his wife Yaichi's condition improved. A month after that, he recovered to almost perfect health and was able to work in the fields. Taeko never stopped giving thanks to her ancestors.

23
GLASSES

Eldest daughter Hisako, worked at Hiroshima's *Shinkin* Credit Union Bank, which was 500 meters from *ground zero*. At the time of detonation, the bank's employees had been commuting to work. None of them returned home.

Because of washing the twin's diapers, Hisako had been running late leaving her house for work. Had the twins, deemed *children of good fortune,* saved Hisako's life by virtue of their diapers?

The credit union now had a new building. Hisako returned there and became whispered about as *the sole survivor.* The same was whispered about her father, being the only remaining person of the city's labor service, thanks to his tea break on the way to work.

However, not whispered, but spoken out loud, was the *miracle of miracles.* All ten of the Nakamura family, though within two kilometers of *ground zero,* had withstood the sleeping giant's wrath, the Enola Gay's delivery, and J. Robert Oppenheimer's invention.

The Nakamura family, indeed, all the families, now lived in a new world. Though heard or not, Oppenheimer's words of: *"Now I am death; the destroyer of worlds,"* would be in everyone's lives from Hiroshima on.

Yet, the world would continue on and grow, thanks to the continued attraction between men and women. Not even the negative power that was unleased in 1945 could stop matchmaking, dating, marriage, and children.

At age 22, Hisako, though beautiful with men interested in her, was reluctant to even consider marriage.

Hisako said:

"Seeing how my father had suffered from the effects of atomic radiation, I was worried that I might encounter the same thing someday. If I got married, how could I take the responsibility of a newborn child? We all believed that radioactivity would be passed on for generations, and that a malformed child would be born to those that had been the first to be exposed to its harm.

"I also heard people saying that Hiroshima, which became a burnt field, would not grow any vegetation at all for the next 75 years. Some rumors insisted the aftereffects of radioactivity would continue forever.

"In fact, in the spring, eight months after the bomb fell, I did see with my own eyes, plants growing. But I believed the negative rumors as they were backed up by the devastation that I had also seen with my own eyes. Try as I did, I could never completely wipe out that anxiety from my mind. I believed that us victims of the atomic bomb were in hell if they died.

And in hell if they survived. How could I think about marriage with that kind of mind?"

Despite Hisako's view on *after-bomb marriage,* a lady matchmaker came calling, hoping to successfully introduce and uniting her with a marriage partner.

Though still reluctant to wed, being the oldest, and timing to be considered, Hisako agreed to at least meet with whoever the matchmaker had in mind for her.

As is the custom, the intended was brought to the Nakamura's home and introduced to the family. Akira Okawa was a pleasant looking young man whose glasses made him look intelligent, which time would show him to be. Most important, he had a substantial and secure job.

In 1950s Japan, about 70 percent of all marriages were arranged. In those days, possible partners met, accompanied by the matchmaker, to size each other up. It often felt like business partners working out a deal. If the couple liked each other, and if both families thought their union was advantageous for all, the couple dated until their engagement was formally announced and gifts exchanged.

At that time, love was expressed more by gifts than by words because love was traditionally regarded as a disruption to social harmony. An emotion that leads to bad ends. For example, Japanese literature has many passionate stories about geishas and their loves committing double suicides.

To the contrary, for Hisako and Akira. They married and had a happy first year together with their second year welcoming a son named Motoyuki.

Akira was in charge of railroad construction for the *Japanese National Railways*. In their second year of marriage, during a downpour of rain, Akira inadvertently decided his own fate.

Hisako said:

"In case of stormy weather, my husband's railroad construction would shut down. However, due to the construction of a special railway bridge, the construction deadline was coming up. So, some of the foremen went to work in the bad weather.

"Because Akira was in charge, he suddenly decided to commute to work right away saying, 'I can't let my subordinates work alone.'

"I thought he'd be staying home, so I had nothing prepared for him to take to work. So, I quickly put some green onions and *umeboshi* plum pickles on barley rice into his lunch box, gave it to him and saw him off.

"Just after noontime, my doorbell rang. When I opened the door, I saw one of Akira's company colleagues standing there with a terribly sad face. 'There's been an accident,' he said. 'Akira San has been taken to the hospital.'

"Not thinking that it was a big accident, I went into our bedroom to pack a robe and slippers for him. But my mother-in-law who was living with us said, 'Forget that, go right now.' So I did, driven by my husband's co-worker.

"When I arrived at the hospital, they guided me to a room where I saw a man lying on his back. I wasn't sure if it was Akira. I hoped it wasn't. The man's face was covered by a white cloth. But I recognized his clothes and knew it was his room that they had taken me to. It was Akira. I leaned over and put my arms around his body and cried.

"I was told later that Akira was involved in the construction of a bridge on the *Sanyo Main Line*. He was standing below the bridge when a steel girder fell on him. He died instantly. I was exposed to the atomic bomb, yet Akira, who I loved deeply, died before me. The irony of it all made me think deeply.

"Why had I overslept just that one time during the three months that I had been working, missing being at ground zero? Why had Akira gone to work instead of staying home? Why was he under that bridge at the exact moment, in the exact place, where the girder fell? Why wasn't he standing just three safe meters from that spot so he could survive?

"I thought my life had ended that day of the atomic bomb. However, I was saved, got married, came to love Akira, had a child, and had two enjoyable years of married life. And now, once again, my life had ended.

"I thought about the stories I had been told about my grandfather Kichizaemon Wada who gave his whole life to helping people. *If this is the end of my happiness*, I thought,

*then from now on, with Kichizaemon watching over me, I will
live for the Nakamura family."*

Though remaining a beautiful woman who received much
interest and marriage proposals from four different men,
Hisako remained single and dedicated to her family. Thought
the years, her siblings would refer to her as *'the hero of the
Nakamura family.'*

In her elder years, relatives were helping Hisako clean up
her home. A pair of glasses were found and were about to be
thrown out. "No," Hisako said. "Those are Akira's glasses. I'll
always keep them. I still pray for him every night."

PART FOUR

MONEY

A medium of exchange that functions as legal tender.

24
STEEL

The war had been over for three years. Everyday living was now feeling calmer. Father Yaichi had now healed up, thanks to his wife Taeko getting him to the experimental treatment and also due to her nursing him.

Taeko had also regained her energy. She always had concerns for the return of radiation problems but kept those in the back of her mind so she could make things for her family as good as possible. She knew that sometimes cultivating the fields around her garden would not always yield the needed food for such a big family. Eight children still had years to go before they would leave their home, so Taeko and Yaichi continued talking about the steps they needed to take for their family's financial future.

As they grew up, identical twins Hiroko and Aiko had similar faces and body shapes, but their personalities were opposite. Hiroko always had an innocent personality, a free-spirited artist who later enjoyed painting. Aiko, on the other hand, was a conscience type who did her best to help her family and others.

Aiko said:

"I grew up being told by my parents and others that it's all right for twin sisters to express their own individuality. Hiroko and I do have different personalities, but that difference actually made us closer than if we were similar. We never had a fight. And we needed each other because of our different temperaments. We overlapped and filled each other's gaps, one complimenting the other. We knew that we would always be connected, even if we lived apart."

Now that the family was healthy, Yaichi decided to start a business that didn't depend on food from the fields. The best way to do that would be to revive the sewing needle-making mill which they were forced to abandon because of nuclear fission. They decided to build a small mill next to their house to start producing needles again. Taeko knew that her husband was good at business, so they had a chance to succeed.

Yaichi knew that the three elements necessary for a healthy human life are food, housing, and clothing. The citizens of Hiroshima had lost most of all three of those elements. They were desperately seeking food and shelter. Next comes clothing. And that's where the demand for needles was. And that demand would soon increase quickly.

Yaichi, who was dexterous and good at making things, was engaged in needle-making since before the war. His skill was highly respected by others in the industry.

To this day, Hiroshima is still where needle-making is popular. Sewing needles manufactured there are called *Hiroshima Needles*. They spread from there, not only through Japan, but all over the world. Though devastated by the atomic bomb, needle-making revived powerfully after the war and thrives to this day.

All this started when, hundreds of years ago, a craftsman named Jizaemon Kiya came from Nagasaki to teach his unique needle-making technique. That teaching was passed on to lower-level samurai in Hiroshima. Needle-making for samurai uniforms was encouraged by the feudal Lord Satoshi Asano.

The development of needle-making in Hiroshima is also largely due to the blessings of the land. It was easy to obtain iron, which is the material for needles. The Chugoku Mountains behind Hiroshima is a major iron sand producing area. That sand was transported to Hiroshima by boat on the Ota River.

Tatara ironmaking is a method that has been around for a long time in Japan. Simply put, iron sand contained in earth, is processed with the high heat of charcoal, and then reduced to make iron.

The Chugoku Mountains were blessed with high-quality iron sand and forests for making charcoal as a thermal power source to reduce it to iron. This has led to the development of a major steel industry in this area.

At that time, there was one of Japan's largest ironmaking companies called *Sumiya* in Yamagata-gun, who lived in a mountainous town in Hiroshima Prefecture. The iron produced there was transported to Kabe by boats on the Ota River. And then from Kabe to Hiroshima castle.

Because of these geographical conditions, Hiroshima needle-making developed as a local industry. However, needle-making 200 years ago was just a small handicraft. At that time, the leading production areas for needle-making were mainly Kyoto and Osaka, which also had a large kimono culture area.

The sudden expansion in needle production in Hiroshima was triggered by the First World War (1914-1918). Due to this war, the production of needles was interrupted in various European countries, so special demand came to Japan. Not missing this opportunity, the needle makers in Hiroshima quickly set up a *production increase system* and expanded its sales channels to Europe. That's how Hiroshima made a sudden jump to become one of Japan's leading needle-making production areas.

When Japan entered World War ll, steel, the material used for needles, was in short supply. However, needles were necessary for sewing military uniforms. Hiroshima needles were manufactured as best they could, supplying 90% of Japan's demands. Riding on that wave, Yaichi Nakamura founded *Nakamura Hari Seisakusho* in 1941, to produce needles. However, the family's needle mill turned to rubble in a blinding flash, four years later.

25
BRAINSTORM

Hiroshima had suffered incredible damage, but the reconstruction moved forward at a good speed. The same was true for the needle manufacturing industry. Needle producers, who had been evacuated, returned to the city to continue making needles.

Hiroshima Prefecture encouraged the production of traditional needles, as each needle factory started to get up to speed. However, many needle-making technicians had died in the atomic blast, so the needle-making industry ran into problems with workers who could not make good needles. Even though production increased day by day, the quality declined significantly.

Because of that lower quality of product, many needle wholesale companies, that had a good reputation for hundreds of years had no choice but to temporarily close their businesses in the name of *goodwill* and *conscience*. However, by March of 1946, the needle-making business in Hiroshima began to rebound to their prewar output.

Then, other manufacturers started their business and gradually regained their prewar activity, even with the serious shortage of labor. So, the time was ripe for Yaichi Nakamura to quickly rebuild his needle mill and resume the production, even in small amounts.

In an era when postwar clothing is not satisfactory, needles come in handy at home as a daily necessity. Also, with few doctors at that time, first aid kits containing cold medicine, wound medicine, bandages, etc. were always kept in each household. Sewing boxes containing various needles, threads, scissors, etc. were also needed household items.

Even though it was a needle-making industry, most of it was still manual work at that time, far from being mechanized.

Hiroko remembered:

"A female worker at our needle mill melted a glass rod on the head of the needle and glued a ball to it. That required good speed and craftsmanship. A needle is an inexpensive product, so you can't spend much time and money on the process. I remember my father being absorbed in his work. He had great patience with the workers and had skills of his own. He received orders from major needle-making companies, so our female workers often increased.

"With larger numbers of orders coming in, my father worried about the inefficiency of workers putting the heads on the needles. He wanted to mechanize it. The automation of sewing needles was done by machines imported from Germany and other countries. But the only way to put heads on the needles was by human hands."

When Hiroko and Aiko, were in elementary school, they found a plastic bag flying in the wind on their way home. The twins chased it. The plastic bag flew around surprisingly quick, so they couldn't catch it easily. It became a competition to see which one of them could grab it.

Finally, Aiko caught it. When she put her fingers inside, it was clean, clear and could see her fingers easily. They took the bag home and used it to store their marbles in it.

Aiko said:

"We used to put our marbles in a paper pattern box. But when we put them in the transparent plastic bag, we could see the colorful glass marbles easily. They looked so beautiful that we put the bag on the shelf so we could always see it.

"When my father saw the plastic marble bag, it gave him an idea. The vinyl was transparent and impermeable to water. The surface of the bag was soft so it would not damage the cloth used for sewing clothes. So he thought: *Isn't it possible to make use of this material for the head of the needle?'*

"The work of female workers had been melting glass rods with fire and attached glass balls to pins by hand. It was very time-consuming and not profitable. It would be better to have this process automated."

Yaichi finally set his sights on this mechanization. A machine that coated the head of the needle with a colorful vinyl. Because it is vinyl, he could freely arrange colors, patterns, and shapes, creating a truly epoch-making needle.

To make that happen, his current small mill building needed to be rebuilt as well as a machine designed and built from scratch. Yaichi dreamed that it would be a completely new method for manufacturing needles.

Once he got that idea, the number one deterrent to all entrepreneurs raised its ugly head … money.

26
WIND

The Nakamura family had lost everything because of the atomic bomb. As always, they had ten mouths to feed and ten bodies to clothe. So, they had no reserve money to use on a business venture such as a needle-making machine.

Asking a bank for a loan would be useless. Bankers wouldn't listen to Yaichi's dream of making a new machine. It would be too risky for them. Dream over. The prosperity for the Nakamura family ... over.

There's a saying: *It's a real bad wind that doesn't blow at least one person some good.*

Maybe a bad wind wasn't responsible for the falling steel beam that crushed the life out of Akira Okawa, but it did blow some good for the ten people.

Around the time that father Yaichi was needing cash to build his needle-making machine, his eldest daughter, Hisako, had lost her husband. Fortunately, the *Japan National Railways* had compensation insurance on him: 500,000 yen (US $600,000 now).

With that money, Hisako had to decide what course of action to take. She wanted to return to her family in Hiroshima, but knew that doing so, she would have to leave her son behind with her husband's parents. She hated to do that but knew she had responsibilities with her parents and siblings.

She did, in fact, leave her son with her in-laws, giving them about 150,000 yen (US $180,000 now) of her insurance money to raise him. Over the years, she would secretly visit him.

Hisako returned to the Nakamura family house with 350,000 yen in her purse. (US $420,000 today). She kept half of that for herself and gave the rest to her father Yaichi to expand the Nakamura needle business. With that money the needle-making mill was rebuilt, and a needle-making machine produced. The mill was operated by his eldest son, Tamotsu, who was then age 25.

Hisako used her credit union experience to handle the business accounting. She also handled the accounting for the Marui Shokai grocery company to make extra money.

After graduating from high school, Yutaka, the second son, joined the family business. The family happily worked hard together and gave thanks for their new prosperity with the needle mill.

In 1950, with the beginning of the Korean War, Japan's economy was booming with special demands for sewing needles. Yaichi's rebuilt needle-mill got off to a good start and developed on the wave of postwar reconstruction. The needles manufactured by the needle-making machine invented by

Yaichi had a good reputation, so orders for needles constantly came in. Orders, not only from Hiroshima, but from Kyoto and Osaka, which were the center of the sewing needle commerce.

Especially popular were pearl-coated pins that were fashionable and elegant. There was a high demand for them for portable sewing kits used in various hotels.

Yaichi said:

"I was surprised to be contacted by a millionaire in Hong Kong. He asked me if I could sell him a needle-making machine for 20 million yen. (US $2.5 million today). I told him, 'If I sell it to China, it will be mass-produced, and my market will be ruined.' So I turned him down.

"My family and I continued to work hard at the mill. Even though tiring, it was fun."

27
SKY

In 1955, Shintaro Ishihara's *Season of the Sun*, became a bestseller. It's a novel about the rebellious youth culture which emerged after the war.

In 1956, the phrase '*It's no longer after the war*' appeared in the newspaper about the *Growth and Modernization of the Japanese Economy*. The phrase became popular, and people tried to live it.

The children of the Nakamura family grew up, and the prosperous family entered an era of what they called '*income doubling*'. However, for them, *forgetting the war* did not mean forgetting the memory of that abominable atomic bomb.

Born five months before the atomic bomb was dropped, the identical twin sisters, Aiko and Hiroko, had a poor life after the war, but had been carefully raised by their parents, brothers and sisters. They had no idea that they were thought by other Japanese people as '*unhappy children*' born under the atomic bomb. It is not because they grew up innocently, but because the family treated and raised them so that they would not feel any such unhappiness.

The twins had always been together since they were born and were close friends. The two shared everything. It's normal for brothers and sisters to fight over something they want, but they naturally shared everything. It wasn't that one of them had the upper hand or that one of them had to put up with the other. They naturally recognized each other's existence and understood each other.

Often, Yaichi put the twins in his bicycle basket and rode them around the town. The two were happy to tour the area that way. Where vacant bombed-out lots used to be, new buildings would appear almost monthly. Flower shops, drug stores, and candy shops would put up new signs, one after another.

Aiko said:

"One time, my dad parked his bicycle in front of a new bakery, went in and bought us some fresh *anpan,* which is a bread roll with sweet bean paste in it. A dream food for children. Right away, my sister Hiroko flattened the two of them between her hands making one large one. Then she put it in the bicycle basket. When we got home, I found out that my *anpan* had disappeared. She had eaten both of them. I didn't mind, but from that time I called her '*Iron Belly.*'

"Identical twins are closer to each other than ordinary sisters, even closer than fraternal twins. My mother told us that identical twins are like splitting one in half, and each other's hearts are the mirror image of the other. The good and the bad in each are equal. The two see themselves in each other. The words and actions of the other twin are also the words and actions of oneself. So I figured that my *anpan* bread was also Hiroko's bread. If I quarreled with Hiroko about it, I would be quarreling with myself."

In 1958, the twins went on to Hiroshima City Nakahiro Junior High School. It was about a 10-minute bicycle ride from their house.

Aiko said:

"We went to school by bicycle and enjoyed being sent off by our mother. Riding through the streets in the morning with the wind blowing our hair was wonderful. Arriving at the school, we saw the many cherry trees that were planted in our school playground."

The twins held hands as they passed through a tunnel of flowers in full bloom at the school's entrance, taking their first step into the *adult world* without any hesitation. An *adult world* because junior high school students who grew up in Hiroshima, were already adults. So, this was the twin's first step into that mature world of peer competition.

On the way back home, the two often went off the regular road and went home along the Ota River. They would lie on their backs on the green grass of the riverbank and look up at the blue sky. They felt like they could stay there forever.

One day in the summer, an airplane appeared like a dot in the distance of the blue sky. It slowly approached and grew larger, making bright white streaks in the sky, then disappeared beyond the mountains.

Aiko kept looking up at the white streak that the airplane left in the sky. To her it looked like the trail of something gone and long forgotten. "During the war," Aiko muttered softly, "did the B-29s bring white streaks like that?

"No," Hiroko answered. "Those stupid B-29s brought the bright light, the black clouds, making the black rain that caused the *pikadon*. Why do you ask? You've heard about it many times."

Aiko was a little confused by Hiroko's unexpected strong tone. But she replied gently, saying, "Yes, I remember all those stories about the people that died with the bomb. And how they were gathered here on the riverbank, piled up like hills, and then burned."

Though the two of them had hardly talked about the bomb until then, they had indeed heard many such stories.

"Lying here like those piled up people," Hiroko whispered, "suddenly feels very morbid." She jumped up quickly, then started running, repeating, "Oh, my god. Oh, my god."

Aiko jumped up and started running after her. If they had been viewed from a distance, they would have looked like innocent children playing tag, instead of girls facing adulthood and the horrors that the world could deliver suddenly without warning.

Luckily (or not luckily), the twins had experienced the Hiroshima tragedy when they were four months old, so they had no direct memory of the terror that the bomb had unleashed. But as they grew up and had more opportunities to interact with Hiroshima families, schoolteachers, and shop owners, the stories they heard about people's misery had piled up in the twin's minds like the bodies at their favorite beautiful river.

Aiko often went to a local bean shop where a beautiful young woman worked with an older woman. The young woman always greeted Aiko with a smile saying, "The Nakamura family sure likes beans."

Aiko would always smile back and say, "Yes, we sure do."

However, the woman's smile began to fade with every visit to her shop. Then her skin slowly turned dark, and pimples started spreading over her face.

One day, coming to pick up beans, the young woman was no longer there. "Where is my friend?" she asked the older woman.

"*Pikadon* poison," the lady said calmly. "She was engaged to be married ... however ..."

Aiko said:

"We had a playmate in my class that started losing his hair and then one day never came to class, nor did he ever come again. There was no explanation from our teacher, but it was rumored that he had moved somewhere with his parents. However, Hiroko and I, and I'm sure other classmates, suspected the truth.

"One by one, classmates disappeared with no word about their absence. It felt like they were *spirited away* and remembered like pictures in a book I'd read a long time ago. Each time that happened, Hiroko and I had vague fears of what the effects of lingering radiation might have on us.

"One day, our teacher showed the class a picture-story of what happened when the atomic bomb hit our city. Hiroko and I had a hard time falling asleep that night. When we told our mother about it the next morning, she said, 'Don't worry about it. Your great-grandfather Kichizaemon Wada will watch over you, so don't think about the atomic bomb. Just study hard at school.' Amazingly, we quickly forgot about the bomb and went out to play."

Hiroko said:

"Later on in high school, when Aiko and I would look up at the endless sky, we were able to forget about the hateful sky with B-29s loaded with atomic bombs. Instead, we saw a *dream sky* that stirred up the romance of travel.

"We wondered how far that airplane would go, and to what fabulous place would it land. We wanted to be on that plane and see the world."

"However, at that time in Japan, people could not travel abroad easily. Even if they could, it would cost more than a luxury car. So, it was unthinkable for ordinary people to have a dream of going to foreign countries. Yet, we continued to dream."

PART FIVE

DREAM

A cherished aspiration, ambition, or ideal.

28
ENEMY

Hiroko and Aiko graduated from junior high school in 1957. Instead of entering a traditional high school that prepared students to attend a university, the twins were sent to a *commercial trade-school*. They were disappointed because they wanted to know more about the world and study those kinds of topics at a regular high school. But their father, who had a craftsman's attitude, had a habit of saying, "Women don't need to study." He thought they should study a trade and get regular jobs.

Hiroko said:

"At that time, I should have studied English more, instead of wasting time with uninteresting bookkeeping and business studies. However, learning to type was good, because when the computer came out, I could use it right away. So, I guess no study is in vain."

During trade school, the twins knew they were no longer satisfied with bicycling around their small town. There was a big world out there that they wanted to experience.

Surprisingly, the Nakamura family was somewhat familiar with overseas because their second daughter, Shizue, had gotten work as a typist at a US Air Force base in Iwakuni. The train was not yet electrified yet, so she went there by steam locomotive. The round trip took more than two hours, so she stayed at a base dormitory for workers.

On weekends, she returned home bringing back stories she had heard from soldier on the base. And sometimes bringing back American gifts she purchased there. Shizue talked about how amazing America is, as the twins soaked up every detail about fashion, products, food, and exciting lifestyle stories. This got the twins' hopes up high to someday travel overseas.

Besides the stories that Shizue told, her own lifestyle was exciting to the twins. In 1949, Shizue graduated from high school and started working at the Air Force base. It was originally a Japanese military base, built before the war, as an education and flight training base. After the war, the American military took over.

At that time, the United States was still considered the enemy that had dropped the atomic bomb on Hiroshima, so it was unthinkable to work for the occupying military. But Shizue not only dared to work there, but she also had a strong desire to get to know the United States positively. She had been inspired by what she had learned about America in the post war years.

Working at the base for ten years, Shizue's connection to America strengthened when Marilyn Monroe's movies *Niagara, Gentlemen Prefer Blondes* and *How to Marry a Millionaire* began showing, both on the Air Force base and in Japanese theaters.

On February 1, 1954, Monroe, with her new husband baseball great Joe DiMaggio, arrived in Japan via a Pan American B-377 Stratocruiser.

They had accepted a three-week *Japanese Baseball League* tour invitation with their schedule put together by the *Yomiuri Shimbun* newspaper. They stayed in Tokyo's Imperial Hotel where crowds of Japanese fans would not leave until Monroe came to her window and waved.

"I felt like I was a dictator," Monroe said.

Before heading out to support the troops in South Korea, Monroe first visited wounded soldiers back from the Korean War recuperating in Japan. On February 11th, she visited the Iwakuni Air Force base where Shizue was working. One can wonder if Shizue saw Monroe's caravan of cars and Jeeps as they arrived on base. Perhaps Shizue even got a glimpse of the movie star herself.

In any event, Shizue, had already enhanced her beautiful face with a Monroe-style hairdo. And had enhanced her sexy figure with tight skirts and sweaters. So, long before Monroe arrived in Japan, Shizue had been tagged with the nickname *Marilyn Monroe*. Soldiers would stop, stare and whistle when she delivered her typed reports from one building to another.

After working ten years at the base, at age 28, she got romantically involved with an American soldier who asked her to get married.

Shizue said:

"When I told my parents that I wanted to marry an American and would go with him when he returned to his country, they reacted like he had personally dropped the bomb on our town. They really rebelled against the idea. To them, even the average American was still a soldier, still the enemy who destroyed their home, burnt the fields, and killed so many. All our neighbors still felt the same way.

"I understood their reaction completely. My father, Yaichi, had suffered greatly from the radiation and his health problems still lingered. 'Marry anyone you want, but not an enemy soldier,' he told me strongly. I didn't argue. I just said, 'I'm getting married to him'."

Ordinarily, Shizue had a calm and quiet demeanor. However, on the day of detonation, it was Shizue that ran to the house to search for the twins, even though her mother thought it was hopeless. Even though Shizue thought more bombs would soon fall, she bravely took action to save her baby sisters.

"Do you really want to go to a country whose people dropped the atomic bomb on us?" her father questioned. "You know they killed thousands of Japanese people, and yet you can tell me this with a calm face?'

"Yes, I'll go with him when he leaves," Shizue replied quietly.

"You don't know how bad it will be for you in America,' he said. "Once you get there, you'll find out quickly."

Shizue said:

"Even though he kept warning me, it didn't matter. The war between our countries had finished. Even Japanese soldiers did terrible things to our own people. The armies of both countries became irrelevant to me. With people, everyone is equal. There is no discrimination.

"Finally, my strong determination wore my parents down and they gave up trying to dissuade me."

A few months later, Shizue Nakamura crossed the Pacific Ocean and became Shizue Frazer. She was one of approximately 50,000 Japanese women who moved to the United States with their GI husbands after World War ll. At that time, it was the largest-ever migration of Asian women to America.

Shizue lived happily in Los Angeles till age 90. The radiation she was exposed to on that horrible day never did catch up with her.

29
TRAVEL

Besides the big event of Shizue's marriage in 1959, there was another important event that would have a decisive impact on the future of twin sisters Hiroko and Aiko. December of that year marked the beginning of the TV program *Kaoru Kanetaka's World Journey*, the first Japanese program about foreign countries.

The host of the show, Miss Kanetaka, traveled with her TV crew filming the customs, culture, and history of countries around the world. Over the years, they visited over 140 countries and accumulated enough flying miles to go around the world 180 times.

Miss Kanetaka conversed with all types of people, from heads of state to villagers in unexplored regions. She even interviewed President Kennedy alone on that program, surprising not only the Japanese, but also the world.

That same year, the number of TV sets in Japanese homes doubled, from one million to two million sets. One of those homes that saw the arrival of a new TV was the Nakamura's.

However, when Miss Kanetaka's show started, it didn't go nation-wide. The neighboring prefectures of *Okayama* and

Sanin Shimane broadcasted it from the first show. But for some reason the TBS broadcast, that covered Hiroshima prefecture, did not broadcast the show. Were *the gods of success* keeping it away from the twins to make their goal more difficult? However, the twins could read about the show each week in newspapers and magazines.

Aiko later said:

"Reading about that weekly show about world travel made Hiroko and I more determined to go beyond our mountains, beyond our sea, and fly around the world. The only way that seemed possible for us at the time was to become stewardesses."

Today, the terms are *flight attendants*, *cabin attendants*, *skycap*, or *cabin crew*. But at that time *stewardess* was the only term used.

Aircraft cabin service began in the United Kingdom in 1919. Initially, young boys were in charge and were called *Cabin Boys*. After that, they became *stewards*. When the world's first female flight attendant was hired in 1930, and term *stewardess*, the female form of the *steward*, was used.

In May of 1931, Tokyo Air Transport Co. hired Japan's first female flight attendant. The term *Air Girl* was used. After WWll, the term was changed to *Air Hostess*. The term *stewardess* became popular in Japan in the mid-1950s when propeller passenger aircraft became jets.

However, no matter what term was used for those flying women, Hiroko and Aiko never breathed a word of their ambition to be working aboard a jet plane. They kept that passionate dream a secret between them because at that time, stewardesses had to not only be a certain height and be good looking, but they also needed a large amount of education and world knowledge. So, for two young girls living in a corner of Hiroshima, aiming to become stewardesses in those days, it was a naïve thing to try to accomplish. Hence their silence on the subject.

Most important for their secret dream was learning another language. For the twins' dream of flying to America, that language was, of course, English. Unfortunately, they were not getting that kind of education at the trade school they were attending. Also, a high school education of any kind was not enough. They had to go to a universality.

The most difficult challenge for them was to continue on to a university via a trade school. And once again, the main obstacle for all dreamers reared its ugly head ... money.

For a while, thanks to Yaichi's needle-making machine, the family prospered. But when the Korean War ended in 1953, the special demand for needles decreased greatly. Added to the fact that Japanese society had begun to make a major shift to mass production, a subcontractor for a major needle factory, such as Yaichi, was not in high demand anymore.

The eldest daughter, Hisako, and the second daughter Shizue were both working. Be even so, under those family economic circumstances, the twins could not go to a university.

131

30
ENGLISH

The trade school that the Hiroko and Aiko were attending was a daily grind for them. A grind with no dream job at its end. All the students around the twins wanted to get regular jobs at a bank or city hall. A natural goal for students there, especially for the girls. The twins, however, were thinking about college. But how to get there? One of them going would be difficult. Two of them seemed impossible.

Finally, they confessed their hopes of higher education to their parents. Taeko understood slightly. But Yaichi would not consider it for the same old reason: "Women don't need to study," Yaichi repeated from years ago.

Without the hope of financial support from their father, the twins decided to get jobs at a local company to start earning money for college.

Hiroko started working at *Marubeni Trading Company*, which was enthusiastic about expanding overseas. It had already established as the first local subsidiary in New York in 1951. It was a perfect company to work for as Hiroko's first step to becoming a stewardess.

Aiko was hired by the *Tokio Marine Fire Insurance* company.

Aiko said:

"I thought that being an employee of a major insurance company would help my chances of becoming a stewardess later. Insurance is a job that is deeply involved in the customer's life which are qualities required of stewardess who supports the safety and security of passengers. Hiroko at her company would have the same possibilities as well for similar reasons.

"And if we could not become stewardesses, we thought with these companies having affiliates in America, we might be able to go overseas sometimes for company business. So these were good places to work for both of us. And most important, Hiroko and I continued to study English seriously."

The twins continued to learn that *impossible dreams* should be kept a secret because it will attract the wrath of the non-believers, the jealous, and the angry.

Aiko said:

"One day, and I can't remember how, it got around my company that I would one day quit and become a stewardess. My bad-mouthed boss laughed in my face saying, 'If you become a stewardess, I'll stand on my hands and walk to Tokyo.'

"I wonder if he, or someone in the company, called my father because when I returned home, he started up on me and

Aiko as well saying, 'You two should stop thinking about the ridiculous idea of becoming stewardesses. You should concentrate on your company's business and study accounting and company policy, not English. Local girls will never get to America.'"

Hiroko said:

"We both denied the rumor knowing that having dreams like going to America or becoming an actress or other wild ideas could not be understood by regular people. By that time, we knew that it's natural for people to discourage dreamers.

"As we strive for what we want, people will put obstacles of reality in our way. But eventually, those very people will be swept away by the mediocre adult way of life."

Even though they studied hard, for twins that had survived the Hiroshima bomb, the English words they *never learned* were: *give up, quit, renounce, retire,* or the idiom *hang it up.*

31
BROADCAST

February 1964.

"Ai-Chan," Hiroko called out to her sister. "Look what just happened. A tremendous thing."

Aiko put down her toothbrush and, still drowsy from just awakening, walked into the living room. "You don't need such a loud voice this early in the morning," she said to her twin.

"Look here. Read what it says." She held up the newspaper toward Aiko.

There was a small headline printed on it saying:

Kanetaka Kaoru's World Trip:
Broadcast on Hiroshima TV

The overseas travel program had been well received from the start and had aroused the longings of Japanese people after the war to know about other countries. The show aired every Sunday morning and continue with the same hostess, Kaoru Kanetaka, for 31 years.

Now, finally, the twins could watch it. Or could they? Sometimes a newspaper makes mistakes. Sometimes a dream gets close, then snatched away.

The next Sunday, Hiroko and Aiko sat in front of the TV, eyes nailed to their tiny black and white TV, wondering if the show would really go on as promised.

Their living room clock ticked to 10:30. The TV showed a *Boeing 707* lifting off a runway with the roaring sound of four jet engines. The camera cut to the logo mark of *Pan Am* on the fuselage of the jet.

Pan American World Airways was the sponsor of the show. It had just started its Tokyo-New York flight with the introduction of the state-of-the-art *Boeing 707* jet airliner. It was the first successful commercial passenger jetliner. It started flying passengers on October 26, 1958. A total of 1,010 were built until 1991. It is credited with inaugurating commercial travel in the jet age.

It was Pan Am's Far East District Public Relations Manager, David Jones, that had made the President Kennedy interview possible for the show. The reason is that Pan Am wanted the Japanese route and put all its efforts into promoting it.

Hiroko and Aiko, as well as the rest of Japan, knew of David Jones as something of a celebrity. Four times a year on TV, for 20-years, he awarded sumo tournament winners with the large Pan Am trophy and received an *Award of Special*

Merit from Emperor Hirohito. He was yet another symbol of America for the twins.

That first broadcast for the twins passed quickly. It stirred up longings in them to travel to foreign countries, even more than the stories and souvenirs that Shizue had brought home from the Air Force base. Never missing a show, the 19-year-old twins soaked up every image from abroad, making them more determined to follow their dream of flight.

32
WANTED

Toa Domestic Airways was established in 1953. It was based in Hiroshima and flew mainly local routes. In 1964, the newly completed NAMC YS-11 turboprop airliner was introduced. It was the only post-war plane to be completely designed and manufacture in Japan. With that plane came the need for stewardesses. The company advertised in the newspaper a year later.

Hiroko said:

"This sounds unbelievable, but I was walking past a co-worker's desk at my company when I happened to glance down at his wastepaper box. There, on the top, staring right at me were the words: *Stewardesses Wanted*.

"I grabbed the paper and found out where to apply. I never told my father about seeing that ad in a trash box because he would have said '*It's a bad omen.*' I, on the other hand, saw it as completely opposite: *Something having to do with my dream was thrown away, but I still magically saw it.*

"I think that I would have eventually found out about the search for stewardesses one way or another. But I liked that it happened that way. And besides that, the competition for the available jobs was keen, so it was good that I found out about it as soon as possible."

One can wonder if she knew the words of the great Japanese swordsman Miyamoto Musashi: *"To know what to do, and to take action on it, should be instantaneous."*

Hiroko didn't hesitate. She had worked daily on her goal and was prepared to seize it. Hiroko went through the airline's series of written tests and interviews. The most important 'test' was passing the *'good looks'* test. Passing all of them, at age 20, she became one of Toa Airways' stewardesses.

As expected, her parents, mostly her father, opposed her plan, However, she won them over, because the head office for Toa Airways was in their own city of Hiroshima, with their travel routes mainly in western Japan, such as Osaka and Fukuoka.

Yaichi said:

"First of all, I didn't think my daughter who went to a girls' commercial high school would pass the stewardess recruitment exam, which requires intelligence and education.

"The competition was high because working for an airline was the dream of many young women. However, much to my surprise, my daughter passed all the tests. So then, I became secretly proud of her, and a little later, told her so."

Although the airline company was small and flew only local routes, she was satisfied, knowing that she became a stewardess, which would be a foothold for her next step toward international flying.

Hiroko said:

"Even though my colleagues at the trading company had made jokes and laughed about my dream, they congratulated me and sent me off to my new career with cheers and applause."

A year later, Hiroko, then age 21, transferred to the Indian state-owned airline *Air India*. It flew domestic routes only since 1932, when India was still a British colony. It had been employing Japanese stewardess from their beginning, not requiring them to be university graduates. A high school diploma was sufficient for flying with them if they passed the other requirements. This holds true even today.

Hiroko said:

"At that time, Air India didn't care about a women's education. They judged possible stewardesses for their English conversation ability, charm, and a calm personality that would not get upset. If trouble happened aboard a plane, they wanted us to smile and reassure the passengers.

"That year, I was one of four that was hired by *Air India*. I stayed at a hotel in the port city of Bombay and received training for three months. I saw India, in those days, on the way to and from the airport. I was surprised to see lots of poor and homeless people hanging around everywhere.

"When I first started there, I once gave food to a homeless woman. Then, a man next to her held out his hand and said,

'Give me some, too.' And the many homeless gathered from all directions. Suddenly I was surrounded by a crowd of homeless. I got scared but kept my head down and slowly moved through the crowd and got back to my hotel. I didn't do that again.

"I also remember a long line in front of the train station every day. I wonder what it was for because there were only men standing there, young, and old. When I inquired about it, I was told they were waiting to get a vasectomy to help control the population there. The government was offering a bag of rice to men who would volunteer for that operation.

"Though there were crowds of people there, garbage in the streets and vultures were constantly flying around to raid what food they could find. Strangely, I got used to all of that. After a while, I even started to feel a spiritual charm in India.

"After three months of training, I was able to work on a stopover flight to Hong Kong, flying there from Bombay, India. I stayed at the Hilton Hotel. What a skyscraper it was. I ate dumplings at three in the morning, took a ferry boat to Kowloon Walled City, Hong Kong Island, and Central Hong Kong. That's when I really felt the joy of becoming a stewardess, thinking, *Oh, the world is such a wide place.*"

33
PAN AM

One year after changing jobs to Air India, Hiroko had a chance to step up further. America's Pan Am Airlines, who was co-sponsoring *Kaoru Kanetaka's World Journey*, had begun recruiting Japanese female stewardesses twice a year.

Hiroko applied for the second recruitment exam. Encouraged by her sister, Aiko also applied for Pan Am. Hiroko past the tests and interviews. Aiko passed but was told she would have to lose some weight to comply to Pan Am's standards.

Postwar travel abroad for Japanese citizens was strongly regulated by the U.S. Army General Headquarters. Only foreign travel for work or study was allowed. On April 1, 1964, this regulation was lifted, allowing all Japanese to freely travel, though another regulation confined them to once a year travel abroad.

Even so, it was a giant boom for overseas travel. This was resolved in 1966 when Pan Am began recruiting Japanese stewardesses. With that resolution, anyone could travel to and from overseas almost freely, so the unprecedented overseas travel boom began. At that time, the Tokyo Monorail to

Haneda Airport opened which made getting there easier, faster, and cheaper than by bus or taxi.

Hiroko said:

"That was the year when the door to the world that I long for when seeing *Kaoru Kanetaka's World Journey* program, actually open up for me and Aiko."

Hiroko had just joined Air India in 1966, so she waited for the second stage of Pan Am's recruiting before applying to fly with them. Thousands of applicants rushed in trying to fill the eleven available positions.

Because Hiroko had flying experience with Air India, even though only a year, she had a big advantage over the newcomers. She took the written exams and did the interviews along with ten other young women, and passed through the *narrow gate* to fly with Pan Am. Her next step was to attend the rigorous training school in Miami, Florida.

Hiroko said:

"I flew to Miami from Haneda, Japan via San Francisco. It was the first time for me to step on American soil. Everything I saw and heard was new and fresh. I was amazed at the first large dinner that I had at a hotel in San Francisco. The salad was piled up in a bucket-like container, and the steak was as big as sandals and as thick as a dictionary. That's when I learned that America is giant in every way.

"When I arrived at the Miami training dormitory, I was overwhelmed by all the talented, well-dressed, and beautiful women selected from all over the world. I felt so humbled when I saw them.

"When I entered the room and looked out from the veranda, there were many women in bikinis on the beautiful, white sandy beach. But when I look closely, they are mostly elderly people. They were wearing small, flashy-colored bikinis on their extremely fat bodies. Also, most of them had bright, red lipstick on. I was really taken back by this new culture.

"When I mentioned this to my roommate, she said, 'They sure are different from my mother. It's like living near a monster mansion.' We both laughed."

Classes started with Hiroko constantly learning and being tested in English which was stressful. There were hours of practical training using a mock-up of a jet interior which she enjoyed. She received guidance on how to dress, walk gracefully, apply make-up, and smile naturally.

Hiroko said:

"I was surprised when they taught us how to change diapers. But when I thought about it, I realized that it's a situation that could come up while flying, if a mother needed help with her baby."

Hiroko was only 21 at that time. Some of the women were five years older than her, with many having graduated from a four-year college and flown for other airlines. Because of being the youngest and having an innocent personality, Hiroko loved all her fellow trainees, and she was loved by everyone.

34
FRANCE

"Did you only bring your toothbrush?" the senior purser joked to Hiroko as she stepped aboard her first flight that was bound for Paris.

"Oh, I guess my bag is a little small," Hiroko answered with a smile. Though not completely prepared and worrying about maybe getting a nosebleed because of the air pressure in the jet, she was still excited to serve on a real flight instead of a training one.

Hiroko said:

"I hadn't remembered to bring in-flight, flat shoes. So, I grabbed a pair of large ones by mistake, forcing another Japanese stewardess to use a small pair. She got a little bit indignant, so I gave them back. I ended up serving customers in large fluffy slippers that I carried with me.

"Add that situation to the fact that I was wearing a nose plug because of fearing a nosebleed, I appeared to be a little strange. However, my colleagues smiled because it was my first flight and they could sense my innocent persona, I think."

International stewardesses are assigned a *home base* for living. Hiroko's first base was Hawaii. It had been her dream destination since high school when she saw the Elvis Presley movie *Blue Hawaii*.

In Pan Am, stewardesses could choose their monthly flight routes. Hiroko usually chose a route that would go around the world in ten days. Many westbound routes departed from Honolulu and returned to either Tokyo, Hong Kong, Bangkok and Honolulu. Those routes often laid over in Tokyo giving her a chance to visit her parents.

She also often chose the route from Honolulu to Tonga (West Samoa), Tahiti or New Zealand. "Those were flights where I could enjoy seeing the blue sea and sky of the South Pacific," she said.

"When I flew from Tokyo to Vietnam on a *Rest and Recuperation* flight, it was in the midst of the Vietnam war. I saw the American Secretary of Defense Robert McNamara on board with a concerned face, writing seriously to finish his work before landing.

"I was working in the galley one time when Jackie Onassis (Kennedy) ordered a *short-boiled egg*. I made a mistake of timing and served her a hard-boiled egg. However, she never complained about it, as other people might. I guess she saw me as innocent and didn't want to make me boil another egg."

35
YUJIRO

In the 1960's, stewardesses, especially for Pam Am, were thought to be *Princesses of the Sky*, and in high demand to attend parties and events. In January 1968, her Honolulu roommate happened to meet actor Tetsuya Watari who had come to Hawaii to sail with the even more famous actor Yujiro Ishihara. Watari was taking a vacation from filming the popular TV series *The Outlaw Sword*. Watari's manager invited Hiroko and her roommate to attend a party on Yujiro's yacht.

Hiroko said:

"I'll never forget that time. Yujiro had just finished filming *The Sands of Kurobe* co-starring Toshiro Mifune. They had been an accident while filming a construction tunnel scene. The tunnel was to be flooded with water controlled by the effects men. But suddenly the controls broke, and the flood became real and dangerous. Yujiro and Mifune, along with others of the cast and crew had been trapped in the tunnel. After being rescued they said that they had prepared themselves mentally to die. That incident had been on TV news and in the papers, so I knew about it.

"My stewardess friend Fumiko and I were really nervous when we boarded the luxurious yacht that Yujiro had named *Contessa lll*. There were about a dozen people there, some of them we recognized as Japanese actors. When being introduced to Yujiro, he felt more like a big brother than a movie star because right away his relaxed personality made us feel welcomed.

"Soon we sailed out into the sea with Captain Yujiro at the helm. Later, he walked around the yacht talking with everyone. Even the yacht crew praised their boss's personality, saying, 'Yu-chan is always happy, so it's fun to be with him.'

"The highlight of the cruise was seeing Diamond Head in the sunset before returning to the harbor. As the crew tied up the boat, we saw Yujiro's wife Makiko waiting there to greet everyone and escort us to a beautiful restaurant for dinner.

"At dinner, I remember Yujiro saying about his wife, 'Oh, isn't our Kami-San so beautiful?' The two of them seem like lovers who had just met. At one point in the dinner, looking around at all the happy and prosperous people, I remember thinking what a contrast it was from my childhood in Hiroshima."

36
WEIGHT

Hiroko's twin sister Aiko had spent several years at an insurance company and then applied to Pan Am to be a stewardess as was her dream. As mentioned, she passed both the written tests and the interviews. However, though beautiful, she was slightly over the company's strict weight requirements.

Aiko said:

"I was assigned to work at the airport's Pan Am *Clipper Club* for a while to lose weight, and at the same time to build the muscles and strength to withstand the hard work of a stewardess. *The Clipper Club* served light meals and alcohol for first class passengers waiting for their planes.

"However, the trouble was that the food at Clippers Club was so delicious that I just ate too much and didn't lose weight. In fact, I gained a little.

"So I applied for Cathay Pacific Airways based in Hong Kong and Sabena Airlines based in Belgium. I passed both tests and was a little confused about which one to choose. But in the end, I chose Sabena Airlines because I wanted to fly around Europe more than Asia."

Sabena Airlines was based in Brussels, Belgium. They had expanded their routes to Europe, Africa, Middle East and Far East Asia. They started service to Japan in 1969, requiring them to hire Japanese stewardesses.

Sebina Airline stewardesses often served wearing a kimono with their hair meticulously pulled up, and perfect make-up. Once when Aiko wore a kimono, she changed her socks on the plane and noticed something was strange. The toes on the special kimono socks were on the same side, meaning the large toe of one of them had to go on her little toe and the shape would be bad.

She tried flipping one of them over with the tough bottom part of the sock on top, but that looked worse. She tried to lengthen her kimono to hide her feet but that didn't work. Finally, she decided to wear one sock and to have one bare foot and started serving with a calm face.

"Does your foot hurt?" a woman asked as she was serving him.

"Ah … This is the tradition when wearing a kimono," Hiroko answered seriously.

"Oh, I didn't know that," the woman said with a strange smile.

Aiko said:

"Finally, though working for separate companies, Hiroko and I had achieved our dreams of flying the world. And for both of us, the reality of flying the world exceeded our expectations."

37
DATING

Among the flight routes, Hiroko's favorite city was Bangkok, the capital of Thailand. As the plane approaches, she could see the lush, fertile rice fields of the Mekong Delta, which is long and narrow. Just before landing, exotic pagodas come into view. Though she stayed in many beautiful hotels in other cities, Hiroko was the most relaxed in Bangkok. She felt like she was in another world.

Nowadays, urbanization has progressed, but at that time Bangkok was peaceful. People's lives blended nicely with nature, and time moved slowly like the steady flow of Mekong River. The locals welcomed the visitors with gentle smiles.

Hiroko said:

"In Bangkok, I used to stay at the Pan Am-affiliated Siam Intercontinental Hotel. I felt sentimental when it closed in 2002. The elaborate Thai-style roof was impressive. Despite being in the downtown area, it was a luxurious hotel known for its large garden behind the building where many peacocks roamed naturally.

"One time, I had two full days in Bangkok until my next flight. I was in the hotel lobby looking at books when I saw a man who kept looking at me. He was tall with a handsome face with blue eyes.

"After walking around the hotel as usual, I was absorbed in choosing books at the book stand in the lobby. There was that same man who I was now fascinated by. A tall, nicely proportioned man wearing a fitted, pin-striped suit. I could feel my emotions coming up in me. He introduced himself as Marsh Thomson and after a bit of talking he asked me out on a date.

"I learned that he completed his master's degree at Harvard University and was asked by Hollywood to try acting. However, he became a diplomat for the United States. He had been transferred to Thailand and became so fascinated with the country that when his diplomatic term ended, he didn't return to America. He got a job with a local American company and lived there.

"I was just 22 years old, and Marsh was 38. On our third date he proposed marriage. But it was too abrupt for me because I wanted to fly around the world more, now that I had finally gotten my dream job. I wanted more experiences and challenges before settling down. I told Marsh to wait a year before we got married.

"A year later, Marsh and I registered to be married at the city office in Honolulu where the registrant put a lei of carnations around Marsh's neck and said, 'Congratulations.'

"We flew to the beautiful island of Kauai. I remembered that this is where Elvis Presley sang the song *Kauai, Island of*

Love in the movie *Blue Hawaii*. The movie ended with Elvis getting married there.

"When we walked around a beautiful garden in Kauai, I saw a sign saying: *Stop, Look and Enjoy.* I remember thinking: It's true. In life, we should sometimes stop and live happily in the present. The past is now over. I will live happily with Marsh in the present.

"We had the wedding in a small church in Singapore and then honeymooned in Ceylon Island. Then we returned to Thailand and invited a lot of friends to have a lively reception at a restaurant. That's how my short, but exciting time as a Pan Am stewardess ended. And my life with Marsh began."

38
VIOLINIST

When flying, Aiko met a talented violinist named Thanos
Adamopoulos who played with the Rotterdam Philharmonic
Orchestra in the Netherlands from age 19. He also had great
success as a musician and served as a concertmaster of the
Opera House. He was not only active in Europe but also in the
United States and Asia as a conductor. He took up the post of
professor at the prestigious Royal Conservatory of Brussels.

Aiko married Thanos and had a son and a daughter with
him. They built a happy family life in Brussels.

Hiroko and Marsh moved from Bangkok to Washington because Marsh was appointed as press secretary for Vice President Agnew under the Nixon administration. They lived in Washington for three and a half years. They were blessed with three children in quick succession: Julia, Joshua, and Akiko.

After the Vice President released Marsh, he was assigned to Manila, Philippines, as the head of the Peace Corps where the family lived happily.

39
REUNION

In the summer of 2014, Hiroko and Aiko, now age 69 returned to their parents' home in Hiroshima. The scenery flowing through the train window was not their old townscape. The streets were wider, lined with more trees, with modern clean buildings.

The sliding door at the entrance of their old home rattled open as Hisako, the eldest daughter, who was 87 years old, welcomed them with a big smile.

After the death of their parents, Hisako lived in the house by herself. Her husband's glasses that remained after his accident were carefully wrapped in cotton and kept in a chest of drawers, preserved like a treasure. She guided the twins to the Buddhist altar where the three prayed for a few minutes. Hisako chanted a prayer of protection for the Nakamura family every morning.

Hisako told the twins:

"I am grateful to my ancestors for them miraculously saving all ten of our family during that awful time. I also thank our parents for devoting themselves to raising eight children from the war and postwar turmoil."

Soon, others of the family still living in Hiroshima arrived. Tsuneko, the third daughter, who was the sixth grader, at the time of the atomic bombing was now 82 years old. The youngest son, Yutaka, was 79 years old and was still running his father's needle factory. He hadn't lost his boy's heart and when he speaks of the miserable time of the bomb, it's always in a fun tone. Fumiko, the fourth daughter, who was saved by her eldest daughter Hisako, just before the house collapsed, was 74.

Shizue, the second daughter who married the U.S. soldier and went to the United States, was living in Los Angeles. Unfortunately, this time it was not possible for her to join the reunion. However, she said that she is living happily in America as she dreamed.

The eldest son, Tamotsu, who was deep inside the docked ship during detonation, also worked at his father's needle factory and arrived smiling.

Hiroko's three children also joined the happy reunion. Julia, the eldest daughter, brought Hiroko's two grandchildren. Her son Joshua Thompson came from Massachusetts. Her youngest daughter came in from the Philippines where she lived with her husband.

Later, all of them visited the *Atomic Bomb Dome* and the *Atomic Bomb Memorial*.

Aiko and Hiroko.

The younger generation listened to their relatives tell stories about their survival.

Later, Hiroko and Aiko talked about their lives from the days after the atomic bomb to the present day while relaxing at their home. A home that was rebuilt by their father's hands from the rubble left behind by the bomb.

As their conversation overlapped, Hiroko's words were Aiko's words, and Aiko's words became Hiroko's words. The words resonated with each other's hearts, as if they were talking to themselves together.

"Atomic bombs can't kill people."

"It was said that we couldn't grow vegetation for 70 years, but we are living like this. Children are also jumping in good spirits."

"We got stronger instead of dying from being exposed to nuclear power."

"Well, that's why the Nakamura family's women are the strongest in the world."

"I learned the importance of love and peace, not anger or hatred, when the atomic bomb was dropped."

"We still have a mission."

"What is our mission?"

"Peace. My family are all married to people of different nationalities. We are like the United Nations; we have different nationalities. That's why we work for peace."

"I hope the earth becomes one family like us."

AFTERWORD

The Nakamura family story was featured several times in the Hiroshima newspaper.

Hiroko Nakamura, one of the twins, was a classmate of mine at the Pan Am training school in Miami, Florida, in 1967.

Pan Am went bankrupt in 1991, but when we joined the company, the sun was just rising. Pan Am aircraft, with a marine blue mark, covered all the huge airline routes that spread to 118 cities on five continents.

After finishing training in Miami, Hiroko and I were sent to Honolulu, Hawaii. We were rooming together when out of the blue she said, "I'm an atomic bomb survivor from Hiroshima, and I have an *Atomic Bomb Survivor's Health* card."

"What?" I asked in bewilderment.

"I was one of twin babies who was buried alive, and they thought we were dead. But when my mother poured water on the hem of her kimono and wiped my face, I blinked."

I could not have imagined that she, who was young and in perfect health, had been a Hiroshima survivor. I didn't want to hear about the dropping of the atomic bomb when I was about to fly my longed-awaited-for, beautiful world route. So I didn't respond.

Coming from a mountain village in Iwate Prefecture, which was said to be *Japan's Tibet*, I didn't want to remember my own experience of walking 30 minutes to school in the snow, wearing thin shoes with holes that practically made me barefoot.

It was only 10 years ago, in 2012, that I began to seriously face the reality of the Hiroshima atomic bomb. After I started taking foreign tourists around Japan as an interpreter guide, I started to seriously consider what happened there.

While passing in front of the *Dai-ichi Seimei* Building as a guide for a Saudi family of four, I explained, "After the war, the headquarters led by General MacArthur was located here, putting Japan under American occupation for seven years."

The head of the family, who had been completely quiet until then, continued, "The dropping of the atomic bomb on Japan is absolutely unforgivable. It killed so many people. There is no greater sin one can have."

With anger on his gentle face, those two sentences made it clear to me. I was impressed to find such a pure and understanding person from such a distant country as Saudi Arabia.

Looking back, during my many decades of living abroad, the topic of the atomic bombing often was brought up by others.

In 1970, I was in my Pan Am uniform eating breakfast at a cafe in the Intercontinental Hotel in Paris. A young man sitting next to me asked, "Why are you Japanese working for an airline in the country that dropped the atomic bomb on your country?"

"It's the largest airline," I answered. "And the only way I could travel the world."

Most Japanese, in those days, answered by saying, "It couldn't be helped."

Foreign tourists coming to Japan has surged since President Obama visited Hiroshima in 2016. He was the first sitting US president to do so. A few years ago, the Hiroshima Peace Memorial Museum became one of the must-visit destinations for Americans.

When I guided a tour to the front of the Atomic Bomb Dome, an American woman in the group suddenly put her arm around me and said, "Let's take a picture together as an American and Japanese, to prevent this tragedy from ever happening again"

I was impressed by the strength of her hand that gripped my arm and the solemn look on her face.

Now, every time I visit there, I am reminded of the twin babies who were rescued from the rubble and the miraculous story of all ten family members surviving. It becomes more moving with each passing year.

Hisako, the eldest daughter of the Nakamura family, who took care of Hiroko and Aiko's Japan home while they were living abroad, is still alive and well at the age of 96.

In one corner of Hiroshima, where skyscrapers now line the streets, a small house remains from when the atomic bomb was dropped. It's waiting for the return of the Nakamura twins.

This year marks the 77th anniversary of the atomic bombing of Hiroshima. The first one in the world ever dropped.

The corona crisis, Russia's invasion of Ukraine, and dark social conditions continue. Whenever war breaks out somewhere in the world, there is concern about the use of nuclear weapons.

The only thing that can compensate the victims of Hiroshima and Nagasaki, is the realization of a world free of nuclear weapons. Like the twin sisters Hiroko and Aiko said, "The world is one."

✦ ✦ ✦

About the Author

Fumiko Takahashi flew for Pan American Airlines for 16 years. She earned a Master's degree from Columbia University NYC. She's written 16 books. Her book, *Disappearance: The Rise and Fall of Pan American Airlines,* won her first prize in the Japan *Ministry of Transportation* competition.

✦ ✦ ✦

The Japanese *nihongo* version of *Hiroshima Twins* is available on Amazon Japan.

Made in the USA
Las Vegas, NV
05 November 2022

58840376R00098